Also by Vivian Gornick

WOMAN IN SEXIST SOCIETY: STUDIES IN
POWER AND POWERLESSNESS
(Edited with Barbara K. Moran)

IN SEARCH OF ALI MAHMOUD: AN
AMERICAN WOMAN IN EGYPT

THE ROMANCE OF AMERICAN COMMUNISM

ESSAYS IN FEMINISM

FIERCE ATTACHMENTS

WOMEN IN SCIENCE

100 Journeys
into the Territory

REVISED EDITION

By Vivian Gornick

A TOUCHSTONE BOOK
Published by Simon & Schuster Inc.
New York · London · Toronto
Sydney · Tokyo · Singapore

Touchstone
Simon & Schuster Building
Rockefeller Center
1230 Avenue of the Americas
New York, New York 10020

1 3 5 7 9 10 8 6 4 2

1 3 5 7 9 10 8 6 4 2 Pbk.

Library of Congress Cataloging in Publication
data
Gornick, Vivian.
Women in science.
Bibliography: p.
Includes index.
1. Women in science. I. Title.
Q130.G67   1983   508'.8042   83–4742
ISBN 0–671–41738–X
ISBN 0–671–69592–4 Pbk.

ACKNOWLEDGMENTS
AND ANNOUNCEMENTS

I wish to thank the Ford Foundation for the financial support it extended me while I was writing this book. I also wish to thank the MacDowell Colony and Yaddo for giving me much-needed refuge during this same period of time.

I have changed the names of all the scientists I interviewed, as well as their places of work and residence, and their actual disciplines. However, not one scientist described or referred to is a composite figure. Each one is her own separate self.

This book is for Naomi Weisstein
—without whom indeed

CONTENTS

INTRODUCTION

Three years ago I read Horace Freeland Judson's masterly account of the discovery of the structure of DNA, *The Eighth Day of Creation*. As the complex discussion of the book moved forward (DNA is the culminating event in the rise of molecular biology; its discovery encompasses fifty years of science), something rare in science writing occurred: the scientists themselves came to vivid and curiously unexpected life. A large number of men and one woman seemed to be wrestling with nature, against themselves, and against each other, not only for an answer to a scientific problem but for a prize, a win, a victory whose nature was complex, not simple. I began to feel a network of human beings moving about inside a profession that had a history, was marked by mysterious influences and baffling hierarchies, and characterized by people with peculiar personalities and neurotic behavior traits as well as by people endowed with nobility of mind and spirit.

How each of the people did science, as well as the revelation that each one did it differently, seemed to be of real importance. Apparently, it was not true that all was subsumed in what is rhetorically called "the scientific process"; sometimes all was, and then again sometimes it wasn't. Concomitantly, professional science seemed to stimulate some scientific workers and to paralyze others. It was not a given that if you were a good scientist you were assured of rising in the scientific world, or even of obtaining a protected niche in which to be productive. There was, clearly, a certain amount of tumult over the matter of professional survival.

But the work itself dominated *The Eighth Day of Creation,* and the extraordinary amount of passionate, single-minded talking, thinking, writing about science that all these people were doing, even as they went crashing into each other (brooding, competing, confiding, distrusting), endlessly conniving and in conflict with the prejudices of their institutions and with the politics of their profession, struck me forcibly.

Two aspects of Judson's packed narrative stayed with me long after I had put the book down. One was the working companionship of Francis Crick and James Watson, the two biologists who solved the problem of the structure of DNA and won the Nobel Prize; the other was the isolation of Rosalind Franklin, the x-ray crystallographer whose observations and photographs contributed crucially to the ultimate discovery.

The relationship between Crick and Watson was its own double helix: all attracting opposites and catalytic joinings. These two ate, drank, slept, and breathed DNA. They were welded together in a richness of obsession that had its own striking life, a life that was a function of the work. It would last no longer than the problem did, but while the problem lasted each of these men felt himself incomparably alive— chained to the other, chained to the problem. I knew even as I was reading that this must be as rare a collaboration in science as it was elsewhere, but I also knew that it was paradigmatic. This, surely, was the meaning of creative force in science.

And then there was Rosalind Franklin of whom Judson very nearly says: If she had had someone to talk to, chances are she would have gotten to DNA first, it was all there in her notes and photographs, she just didn't know what to make of what she had. Rosalind Franklin worked in the same London laboratory of Kings College as did Maurice Wilkins who was also working on DNA, and who ultimately shared the Nobel with Crick and Watson at the Cavendish Laboratory in Cambridge, but Franklin did not work with Wilkins, nor did she work with anyone else in London.

Much in Rosalind Franklin's behavior and identity might account for her severe isolation in the London laboratory. She was considered by many (certainly by Wilkins) suspicious, abrasive, defensive. She was also Jewish, she was not a biologist, in no sense was she in the club, anyone's club. But as I read on in *The Eighth Day* the conviction began to grow in me that woman *qua* woman Franklin was something of a permanent freak in their midst, and that it was this unalterable fact that fed so disastrously into an alienation that might have been ameliorated had she been a man. As a woman, she was a historic stranger in the Kings College laboratory: They had never really had them, never wanted them, never known what to do with them; women in the lab just didn't seem right.

Rosalind Franklin made me begin to think about what it might be like to be a scientist who is a woman. Science is, after all, the pursuit of "the real thing"—the ultimate effort to separate out what is real from what is not. Everyone working in science swears by the accessibility of that pursuit to all who demonstrate themselves intellectually and emotionally fit to make it. But what if a woman working in science feels it is *not* so accessible to her? What then? What does it mean to work in a world where it is asserted that "subjectivities" are without power or influence, and yet such is not the case? What are the clear—as well as the incalculable—costs of being one, or one of a few, among the many? What if a woman in science feels she must prove herself many times more often than a man does; that her work is more often challenged and less often supported; that she cannot get grants, equipment, promotions, and tenure as easily as her male counterparts do; that she works under the peculiar strain of an excluding hierarchy of working colleagues that is always operative and always denied. What happens to her nerve, her self-confidence, her ability to believe in the evidence of her own intelligence? What is the effect on the capacity for creative thought?

I set out with only these few sentences in my head to investigate the atmosphere that had generated such questions, to learn something of what it was like to be a woman in science in America today, and as I thought nothing more telling than a description of the way it feels to those living it out, I decided simply to go to scientists who were women and say to them, "What has it been like for you?"

I narrowed my definition of a scientist down to those who did basic research, and accepted as my subjects biologists, chemists, physicists, physiologists, and experimental psychologists. I talked with women in their twenties, thirties, and forties, as well as women in their fifties, sixties, and seventies. My youngest subject was twenty-four years old, my oldest seventy-eight. I talked with women who worked in industry and in government research institutes as well as in the academy, women who were laboratory scientists at every level from graduate student to research associate to principal investigator.

I spent time with more than a hundred scientists, speaking with them in laboratories, offices, restaurants, living rooms, and on park benches in New York, Washington, Boston, California, New Hampshire, and Illinois. Because of the innumerable clichés generated by sociological analysis (scientists are always the oldest child, the middle child, the youngest child; they have one foreign parent, spent their first six years in bed with rheumatic fever, and were raised either in the upper class or in the ghetto), I was surprised by the range of background, history, and experience I encountered. I found scientists who came from Park Avenue, Main Street, and Tobacco Road; from the intellectual elite and the petite bourgeoisie; from parents who were evangelists, actors, lawyers, scientists, tailors, ministers, and coal miners; from families where they were neglected, abused, and ignored, as well as loved, prized, and nourished. Every kind of bleakness and every kind of brilliant light has poured down on them. They came straight from the cradle to science, they came by a circuitous route that resembled a bohemian writer's autobiographical note. What is true for all of them is a shared temperament of mind and spirit that defies analysis as to its origin but is invariably made substantive in the same way: Each of them had wanted to know how the physical world worked, and each of them had found that discovering how things worked through the exercise of her own mental powers gave her an intensity of pleasure and purpose, a sense of reality nothing else could match. When she put it all together she knew she was a scientist. In each life a different set of circumstances, and a different psychological time span, was required to put it together.

What did I expect to find, and what did I actually find? To state the case quickly: I think I set out simply to document discrimination against women in science. In a profession justly characterized as powerful, authoritarian, and preeminently male, I expected to find their numbers insignificant, their positions uniformly subordinate, their personalities subdued, their minds safely conservative. That expectation did not bear fruit. I have been deeply moved by the resourcefulness of women in science rather than by their victimization, and amazed by the variety of their personalities, their experience, and their activity. I discovered how passionate an enterprise science is—how like artists scientists are—and that hundreds of women who possessed the driving spirit, the pressing hunger, occupied peripheral, often humiliating positions for twenty and thirty years in order to do science. You could not keep them out of the human enterprise, and because you could not keep them out they have created a history, left a legacy, had consequences. Together with the contemporary woman's movement, they have formed a wedge, making the opening for women in science larger than ever before so that today—while the profession is still without anything that resembles parity—innumerable women in science are where they belong, in possession of grants, professorships, and laboratories, and thousands of young women think it perfectly natural that they should become scientists.

I thought I would find most women scientists antifeminist, as one generally does find the women in a profession whose hierarchy often tyrannizes in the name of "rigor of mind," threatening to hurl into the purgatory of professional contempt those fellow workers who hold unorthodox views or entertain perspectives of thought as yet unendorsed by the intellectual heads of state. Instead, I found very few antifeminists among the scientists, a surprisingly large number of open feminists, an even larger number of fellow travelers, and not one scientist in her thirties or forties who did not acknowledge the influence of the woman's movement on her own working life and on the life of professional science.

Generally, when a scientist spoke of the difference the woman's movement has made in science, she was speaking in what we might call "gross" terms—that is, of the increase in grants, tenure, and promotions for women, the alterations in hiring practices, awarding of prizes, inclusions in honor societies. What struck me forcibly, though, in the year I spent with the scientists was the subtler way in which feminism and science had begun to flow into each other in these past years.

There were a number of scientists in their fifties who had lived much of their lives as women for whom being a woman is a profession, and then in their maturity had discovered they had scientific talent and had become scientists. These women embodied a new imperative. One of them expressed it most memorably when she said: "All my life, when I've been asked my opinion, I've said, 'I *feel* . . .' And so has every other woman I've ever known. And that's all right. We haven't done so badly with 'I feel.' But I went into science because I wanted to be able to say 'I think.' " When I came to know this scientist better I discovered that "I wanted to be able to say 'I think' " was a euphemism for "I *need* to think."

Another scientist, a woman of fifty-four, had married at seventeen, raised six children, gone back to school at forty, become a biologist, and was now the principal investigator of a laboratory in an Eastern medical school two hundred miles from home. Her husband had been proud and sustaining all the way through, agreeable to their meeting one weekend a month in either her city or his. Then he was transferred to the West Coast, and suddenly their relationship was thrown into question. "I think Dave was surprised when I didn't follow him to California," the scientist said. "And God, I wanted to. I miss him terribly." She looked down into her lap, then looked up and said, "But what would I do with the rest of my life if I gave up science? I can't stop thinking *now*."

It was through such women that I came to perceive the addictive quality of scientific thinking, to see that it feeds something incomparable: a clarity of inner being which once experienced cannot be done without. These women, these older scientists who had lived whole other lifetimes as the professional lovers of men and children, they knew the value of intimacy in the dailiness of life, they knew the meaning of doing without love, they did not speak idly or in ignorance. But each of them indicated that now, if forced to choose between family life and science, she would have to choose science. Each of them had become devoted to the experiencing self characterized by work rather than love, and had begun to construct her life around that devotion. Love, necessary love, was now at a proper remove.

At the beginning of my time with them I did not know the meaning of the titles that came with the geneticists and physiologists and biochemists with whom I was speaking. I did not know what it meant to be a "post-doc," or a research associate, or a principal investigator. I knew the job descriptions, but I didn't know the meaning. A year later, I understood that if a scientist was a research associate it meant that she worked on someone else's grant in a lab where the problems were set by someone else, that she had no direct power or authority, and was not a scientist in her own right by the dictates of her profession. This did not tell me whether or not she was a good scientist; it only told me she was not professionally successful. Conversely, a woman who either had tenure or was on a tenured track line at an established university or research institute had a grant of her own, was the principal investigator in a laboratory (she set the problems and she paid the salaries), and was certainly a successful scientist. But that did not tell me if she was an excellent scientist, much less a brilliant one.

I soon discovered it was neither excellence nor success that held my deepest attention. What I found most compelling was the sight of people engaged by what they did with an intensity that was transforming. Here was work capable of inducing excitement of the highest order. This human excitement seemed more to the point, and here the matter of being a woman in science was crucial.

The question that had been forming at the back of my mind at last focused. It was this: A female person grows up, discovers that by virtue of temperament, inclination, and talent she is a scientist, and she becomes one. Then what? How much battle must she do to get to the excitement? What is the nature of the battle, and what are the odds that she will make it? Is there flux in the atmosphere? Is she struggling in a static world or a fluid one? In a state of agitation or paralysis? What are the chances of her breaking free and penetrating to the center?

Arriving at the center. I began to see that this was the true subject of my inquiry. I came within the year to see that this question—not even of arriving but of *traveling* toward the center—was intimately bound up with those earlier questions of mine ("What if a woman in science feels she must prove herself more often, is more often challenged, less often supported? What happens to her nerve, her self-confidence? What is the effect on her capacity for creative thought?"); that it was, in fact, what "women in science" was properly about. I remember the moment the insight clarified for me. It was while reading Robert Merton's *Sociology of Science*.

Merton is a thoughtful and systematic observer of the contemporary practice of science. His style is open, friendly, informed. In an essay called "Priorities in Scientific Discovery" (part of the larger work), he describes the striking competitiveness among scientists and demonstrates that throughout history, from Galileo to Einstein, men of meek, even pathologically shy temperament and personality have battled each other fiercely over proper recognition for who discovered what. Merton explains: "In the institution of science originality is at a premium. . . . Interest in recognition, therefore, need not be, though it can readily become, simply a desire for self-aggrandizement or an expression of egotism . . . it is enough that science, with its abiding and often functional emphasis on originality and its assigning of large rewards for originality, makes recognition of priority uppermost. . . . This means that long before we know anything about the distinctive personality of this or that scientist, we know that he will be under pressure to make his contributions to knowledge known to other scientists and that they, in turn, will be under pressure to acknowledge his rights to his intellectual property. . . . the great frequency of struggles over priority (results) from the institution of science, which defines originality as a supreme value and thereby makes recognition of one's originality a major concern." Merton then fleshes out his observation with a series of anecdotes about well- and little-known battles among scientists in the matter of original discovery; these anecdotes are richly suffused with a sense of shared urgency, historic context.

Women scientists reading "Priorities in Scientific Discovery" will recognize the territory immediately. They will know what country they are in, and they will know these figures planted squarely on the landscape. They will "identify" with them in the large way that all human beings identify with shared impulses expressed in a familiar idiom (as girl readers identified with the hero in a *bildungsroman* although they themselves were never going to leave home). But for the majority of women scientists, Merton's description embodies neither actual experience (there is, in fact, not a single woman mentioned in the essay) nor historic expectations. It is not a record of their personal histories in science or of the culture of their working lives.

My scientists most of them, had long ago put one foot across the border into their world—many of them had even taken a single giant step inside the territory—and there they remained, frozen in position, watching generation after generation of bright young men move swiftly past them. They knew as much about being half in and half out as does any serious worker who is a woman, but they knew very little of the taste or feel of open competition. That is not where they have been, or who they have been. If a woman scientist were to sit down and write a history of scientific competitiveness out of her own experience, I doubt that a work of any depth or originality would emerge.

But a woman scientist has been somewhere in science, and she has a particular knowledge of the territory. The world looks different to one who stands on the border advancing only slowly toward the interior than it does to one whose feet have always been moving directly and confidently toward the center. That difference is substantive, and it is worthy of our attention. It is a difference that, of necessity, has hardly been

I was urged by many people—most especially by many scientists—to speak with men in science as well as with women. In order, it was said, that I gain perspective, a balanced sense of what was common to all, peculiar to some. In short, that I make my view respectable by claiming for it the authority of the controlled experiment. I considered the merits of this proposal for a time, and rejected them. What, after all, was to be gained in paying shallow homage to the dictates of social science?

This book is not a comparative study of men and women in science nor is it a statistical survey or a sociological analysis. It is a work of impressionistic journalism reflective of the way I received and interpreted a piece of experience: the stubborn, persistent, painful, admirable advance by some people who are women on the educated and passionate effort to describe the physical world from the cell up.

Six years have passed since *Women in Science* was written. Over these years I've received mail from women of all ages who have thanked me for the book and told me it was gratifying to see their own experiences mirrored in its pages. It is women in their twenties, especially, whose letters have most touched me. They've told me the book helped clarify a puzzling and difficult time for them: the time when they first began to think seriously of doing science and found themselves receiving mixed signals about their welcome into the enterprise. I find myself wanting, more than ever, to put the book into the hands of more young women—high school and college students—who have a talent and a drive for science, and who stand in the open doorway, about to put a foot across the threshold into "the territory."

The modern women's movement is now, properly speaking, two hundred years old; it dates from the publication of Mary Wollstonecraft's *Vindication of the Rights of Woman*, written in the wake of the French Revolution. Every fifty years since that time, the movement has raised its head, opened its mouth, made another effort to be seen and heard. Each time around its partisans have been renamed—New Women, Free Women, Odd Women, Liberated Women—but in fact it is always the same woman speaking and it is always the same matter of which she speaks. While she has had different and specific issue to take—the right to vote, divorce, our property—her underlying message is: Women need to use their minds more than they need to be mothers and wives; not instead of, just more than. That is the real issue, and around it there has collected over these two centuries an immense amount of thought and feeling. *Women in Science* takes its place in this tradition, retraces the struggle, and makes the story of women trying to do science a paradigm of one of the longest revolutions on human record.

The second wave of American feminism is now in a period of quietude—even of setback. After nearly twenty years of noisy activity on behalf of women's rights, one half of the country thinks the revolution's been won; the other half thinks what feminists have accomplished amounts to a drop in the bucket. Such an extraordinary division of viewpoint indicates that whatever changes have occurred, they are by no means clear and indisputable; for many, in fact, the changes are shallow and insecurely held. Certainly, the Supreme Court decision to restrict the constitutional right to legal abortion makes a subtle contribution to the historic reluctance to allow women the free full use of their gifts of mind and spirit.

Behind the idea that it is natural for women to do intellectual work lies a struggle that, at this moment, is far from concluded. The stories that women scientists have to tell are eloquent and illuminating, the context in which they speak still recognizable. Some day, perhaps, their collective tale will *be* history rather than make history. But today is not the day.

New York City

PART ONE

Who Are These People, And What Do They Think They're Doing?

IN the year I wandered among the scientists, my contacts took me overwhelmingly into cell and molecular biology laboratories—where the largest number of women scientists are to be found—to the work of geneticists, immunologists, endocrinologists; to biochemists, psychobiologists, biophysicists, physiobiologists. Whenever I entered one of these labs I felt excitement in the air. Around the biologists was gathered an intensity of expectation, there in every lab, infecting even the technicians. I felt myself drawn in among an army of workers engaged by an immense piece of knowledge just beyond reach, something whose shape they peered at through the shadows of an ignorance they seemed to feel would lift any minute now; that the dissipation of this ignorance would have great consequence was not in doubt. The atmosphere in the lab spoke. It said, "What we discover here today will immeasurably affect the world that is made tomorrow." It was the excitement of people who believe.

I became persuaded that anyone working in a cell biology laboratory was able to feel him- or herself in the presence of large and urgent doings, and I was repeatedly struck by the thought that an individual writer or philosopher or political thinker, working alone at the desk today, may feel very much the same, but these stirrings are not shared by the general enterprise of literature or philosophy or political thought. The shared conviction that a significant idea or body of ideas has gathered in an intellectual idiom, and the collective brain and spirit is being fired anew, is there now in science. To do science today is to experience a dimension unique in contemporary working lives; the work promises something incomparable: the sense of living both personally and historically. That is why science now draws to itself all kinds of people—charlatans, mediocrities, geniuses—everyone who wants to touch the flame, feel alive to the time.

As I write these words an eyebrow goes up on the face of a critic, a historian of science I know for whom the contemporary practice of science is very nearly anathema. She thinks I have got the whole thing wrong. The people in these labs are data collectors, she tells me. There isn't a thinker or poet among them. They're industrial drones, writers of grant proposals, hustlers and insurance agents who know the money is in biology this year, this decade, this part of our time.

"In the last century," this historian says, "physics was visionary. It's why scientists could speak of 'touching God' and become arrogant in their knowledge. The love affair with Einstein was in the visionary tradition. Time, space, and matter: what more profound questions could one address oneself to? What was below or above that? The idea that a unified theory of physical life would be found was the Holy Grail the knights went seeking. In the nineteenth century biology also was an outgrowth of wonder at phenomena. Like so much else then, biology was filled with a sense of plenitude, the majesty and wholeness of nature, the marvel and order of plant and animal life. In the twentieth century this history has become perverted. Physics has lost its visionary quality, and biology has become a parody of the search for a unified theory. Biology is now 'hot,' fashionable, big business, electric with the energy of competitiveness for money, fame, real power. People work endlessly at their small specialty. Fields have multiplied like rabbits. Any large or intellectual view has long disappeared in the data-collecting process that dominates most scientific life."

Another scientist I know, a behavioral psychologist, nods his head in grim agreement with the historian. In a discussion of the origins of scientific thought, phrenology (the idea that certain of one's mental faculties or character traits are indicated by the configuration of one's skull) is mentioned, and laughingly dismissed by the other discussants. The behaviorist demurs, and uses the occasion to make an observation and pass a judgment:

"In the nineteenth century phrenology took its place in a tradition and a line of thinking that honored and developed a wholeness of observation now passing from us. The neurologist was the natural descendant of the phrenologist. An illness occurred, its source could not be traced, the neurologist observed the patient's physiological behavior, and from his observations he deduced. 'The cause of the problem is *this*,' he said. 'The place where it all begins is *here*,' he posited. When the great machines of today were developed the neurologist became devalued, and along with his loss of authority his overall view became useless. Scientists now said localization and function are everything, the general look at the entirety of behavior is useless. So now they insist—this is what neuroanatomists do, for instance—you take a slice of the brain, spend your life with it under a microscope, and you'll understand everything. To this I say nonsense. My view is the polar opposite. What I do is take a piece of the brain away from an animal and then I watch the entire behavior. To do what I do you don't need big machines or expensive equipment. I can do what I do with a Q-tip stick. But this they think unimportant. I can't get funded for this. I have to produce grants that will show the need for the use of big expensive machinery in order to get support. In other words, thinking is out, technique is in."

A young reproductive biologist—one of the discussants—assents politely that intellect *is* perhaps sadly missing in contemporary science. Then she brightens helplessly: "Yes, but technique is *exciting*. To have the technique and not be able to then ask the right question is one thing, but to not have the technique at all is quite another. The development of technique has made a revolution in cell biology."

There is a quarrel going on inside the profession. It is heated, and it is deadly serious. For some the promise of science is palpable, for others it only serves mass careerism. Where one sees intellectual believers at work another sees mere technicians and still another sees philistines and frauds. The disparity in views is alarming, of such a high order as to indicate the cause of the disruptiveness lies elsewhere, well beyond the borders of science itself. And indeed, the participants in this angry exchange reflect the social upheaval out of which it clearly emerges, and of which it is a vivid example.

I do not think that the visionary quality is gone from science; on the contrary, it appears stronger, more widely subscribed to, than ever before in its history. That intent and excited belief in the meaning of science which has been growing steadily for nearly three hundred years (albeit often in severe eclipse) has arrived at a moment of extraordinary fruition. The moment is coincident with the vast eruption of an egalitarian impulse that has had the unexpected power to invade nearly every aspect of the human enterprise, and nowhere more so than in science precisely because of the magnetic power of its current self-belief.

Science, only yesterday characterized by a genteel and integrated intellectualism, today seems filled with the most unlikely candidates for the life of the mind. This "inappropriateness" induces a confusion of belligerence and interest in every quarter. The historian, the behaviorist, and the biologist are each looking at a profession in a state of volatility.

That which feels open, expansive, rich with promise to one feels fragmented, reduced, anxiety-provoking to another. To some a new set of values and behavior is being created that does not yet lend itself to comprehensive explanation; to others the yahoos are in the tribunal. Behind the perspective of the historian and the behaviorist are ranked many scientists between the ages of sixty and eighty who look around at their younger fellow workers and, in voices marked by open bewilderment, inquire: "Who *are* these people? What do they want? Are they really scientists? Scientists as I have always known them?" The reproductive biologist laughs cheerfully and tells them readily who these people are, and what they think they're doing.

Technique has, indeed, brought profound change during this century to the scientific profession; it has altered the character of the practitioner, the atmosphere of the inquiry, even the substance of the investigation. The great machines of the twentieth century have made scientists think things they could never have thought without them. Certainly, in biology the power of the machine is self-evident. In the 1920s quantum physics made chemistry important to the study of biological molecules and out of this importance biochemistry was created, but the development of the electron microscope in the thirties made cellular structure the equal of chemistry, and out of *this* equation the new science of molecular biology was born.

The electron beam—with its extraordinary capacity to "resolve" separate images into single ones, thereby capturing what the beam of the light microscope had lost—revealed the fine structure of cells and tissue, and renewed the meaning of scientific research. If you were uninitiated (that is, not a biologist) and you looked through the scope, the sense of revelation was apparent at once. If you were initiated and understood the meaning of what you were looking at, you experienced a joy from which you never recovered. A passion for the aesthetics of the cell under the electron beam could, and often did, become addictive.

The most intricate details of cell structure were suddenly visible: Membranes, cilia, nuclei, cell organelles of every kind were seen as complex entities in a totality of environment not previously suspected. A piece of animal tissue looked like a picture of the earth from an airplane: an entire continental topography of rivers, islands, mountains, and forests, valleys filled with waving wheat, oddly shaped flowers and exotic plants. The epithelial lining of the human trachea was like a field of wild thistles, the sarcoma of a rat like snowflakes trapped in amber, the lung of a mouse a marvelous sea sponge with delicate fibrous lines woven inside each hollow of the sponge, butterfly sperm were jeweled perfume bottles, the human pancreas a topographical map of upstate New York. Biologists looked up from the scope in amazement: It is not at all as we imagined it to be, not at all. How beautiful it all is, how indescribably beautiful. And how puzzling. How does all this function? What is this flat mass over here? And that intricacy over there? And over here, this peculiar tubular structure? And here, this string of black beads surrounding the nucleus? And the mitochondrion, what's it doing over here, floating in space?

Biology, having been made modern by quantum physics and chemistry, now became a high-powered analytic science instead of the descriptive one it had been, and began the investigations that would deliver into the second half of the twentieth century a framework for answering some of the great questions of nature, as well as producing an enormous volume of scientific unknowns. Enzyme secretion, hormone action, protein synthesis, energy distribution—how did it all work? What was the molecular structure of a protein? Of an *anything?* We know nothing, nothing. What joy. We know nothing. Everything lies before us.

Then came the realization that the chemical substance DNA was what the human gene was actually made of and in 1953, with the discovery of the structure of DNA, the further realization that all genes, not only human ones, are made of DNA. More joy. Joy for a thousand years to come. Detailed understanding of what biologists call "gene expression" lay spread before generations of scientists. Each separate cell has all the information necessary to create the entire organism; the human nose cell, for instance, carries all the cells necessary to create a whole human being, but in a nose cell all cells except nose cells remain unexpressed. Why? What is happening? How does a gene determine which cell must become a muscle or a nerve—and, at that, a liver muscle, an arm nerve? How does the body *know* how to reproduce its very own self—and not some other animal or plant self—every twenty-four hours? What exactly is it that prevents a human being from waking up a carrot?

It was the technology that produced such questions, and each question produced a hundred more. These questions then, of necessity, irritated into existence more and even better technique so that more exact laboratory conditions could be created under which to study the questions: delicate instruments with which to slice tissue ever more thinly, finer lenses to place in more powerful machines, superior fixatives with which to hold cells on slides, a perfection of tissue-culture medium in which to keep cells alive in the laboratory, or grow them artificially. Many scientists discovered they had a real flair for this sort of thing, and began to fall in love with technique. Sometimes it seemed, almost, that they looked around for a hypothesis on which to hang the technique, so eager were they to use a clever procedure, an inventive piece of equipment.

During these past two decades—due chiefly to the development of the computer—another technological upheaval occurred out of which emerged the neurosciences. As physicists, chemists, and comparative psychologists had come swarming into biological work, now even more of them flocked to brain research, neural anatomy, physiochemistry. Scientific questions multiplied and the development of technique continues apace, often indeed seeming to "outstrip" the process of intellection. It was hard to puzzle the thing out. Was it indeed that thinking was out and technique was in, or was it that a scientist who loved technique had thoughts unavailable to one unfamiliar with technique? Then, was it possible to so consign a scientist either to the sphere of thought or to the province of technique? And, in the end, did it matter? There were, it seemed, enough people to do everything: people to think, people to invent technique, people to work out procedures. Suddenly, there were thousands of people in science.

"Suddenly" began the day World War II ended. The war catalyzed political influences that had been growing for decades, and stirred to conscious life social expectations that would go on expanding until they culminated twenty-five years later in black civil rights, the second wave of feminism, and the popularly held notion that all have the right to "realize" themselves. In the late forties those early not yet articulated expectations met head-on with the excitement and terror induced by nuclear physics, which now told all of us that our description of the world had undergone an irrevocable change. Science called itself violently to public attention. The shared sensibility through which we internalize our common life, and accept the places we occupy in that life, began to transmute itself. A generation would pass before those living it out understood what had happened in that crucial decade, but the felt response was acted upon long before the analysis was in.

Just as technology had grown out of the war, along with

many of the great questions in contemporary science, so the war itself altered forever the terms of educated exchange. Millions of people who before the war would have become white- or even blue-collar workers now, after the war, went to college, got degrees, and entered the professions. Of these millions an enormous percentage would ordinarily have gone into the humanities or the social sciences. Now, great numbers of the enormous percentage set out to become laboratory scientists.

It was exactly like a revolution. Before the revolution, revolution belongs only to revolutionaries, men and women made in a special mold, burning with serious ardor. Afterward, when revolution has become the idiom of ordinary experience, all those who have it in them to do so join the revolution. So it was with science and scientists and World War II.

Before the war scientists were thought of as unsocialized men working, each alone, amidst smoking beakers and blackboards covered with hieroglyphic equations; men who occupied a world of mental construction unavailable to the ordinary intelligence and who were made peculiar by virtue of devotion to an abstraction that compelled even while it isolated. Scientists were an intellectual elect: men cast in a mold at variance with the one in which the rest of us were made.

During the war a significant number of men and women came to realize that doing science was not the mythic other it had seemed from an ignorant distance. Working in hundreds of jobs that required, and thus produced, the ability to solve the technological problems of the most scientifically advanced war in history, many found themselves living daily with scientific method, and employing the scientific process of thought. They were, of course, not scientists as they had always pictured scientists to themselves but, to a surprising degree, they obviously had science in them.

After the war science became a contagious excitement in

the air. It came to embody a transformed attitude toward knowledge and the acquiring of knowledge; rather quickly it was taken as a piece of experience open to public possession. The time of science had come, and thousands of people thought they had every right to take part in that which was timely. An enormous mingling took place. A profession that had been cohesive, homogeneous, and populated in the hundreds now exploded with uncontrollable multiplicity into a pluralism that soon numbered in the tens of thousands.

In the late fifties and early sixties, scientific jobs, positions, titles proliferated. Laboratories and classrooms were built, Ph.D. programs instituted or enlarged. Scientific fields, large and small, grew like wildflowers in an open meadow (the work of three people could constitute a field). New sciences were declared every other year, and scientific societies were formed to validate their existence; there were meetings, conferences, symposia, and journals to publish all their proceedings. And money, money, money. A bureaucracy of grant-givers and grant-receivers sprang up—the same people often occupying positions on both sides of the table, serially and simultaneously. More doctoral degrees in science and engineering were awarded in the fifties than had been earned in the three preceding decades. The number doubled again in the sixties, and grew another 67 percent in the seventies. As of this writing a middle-sized city could easily be populated by workers in the American scientific professions, and certainly it could be supported by the monies that subsidize the enterprise. In 1980 more than seven hundred thousand physical, mathematical, and life scientists were at work in American universities and industry, receiving a large share of the country's total research and development expenditures which came to an estimated sixty-two billion dollars.

In 1953 a psychologist named Anne Roe published a book called *The Making of a Scientist*. Based on carefully designed interviews, Roe's book declared itself a study in the relation between personality structure and scientific work. The text of this book is not interesting (it reads like an unsophisticated sociological survey), but there is a sub-text that is most interesting. The author's unacknowledged attitudes and assumptions, riddled throughout the prose, woven into the syntax, tell much about how a scientist was perceived in the late forties by an ordinarily educated member of the American middle class—that is, a keeper of the culture.

Anne Roe's scientists were all white, all male, and nearly all Protestant (five of the sixty-four were Jews). They were mainly the sons of educated professionals (a few came from the farm and one from the urban ghetto). All were married, very few were divorced. They seemed private, civilized, cheerfully lonely men who often had faced the death of one parent in childhood. Science appeared in this book as a gentleman's profession practiced by the closest America could come to an intellectual gentry.

What is striking about *The Making of a Scientist* is the awe in which Roe holds the scientists—the enormous regard she has for the prestige of their distinguished braininess—and the straightforward, conventional sexism with which she makes it, somewhat regretfully, clear that men alone may be scientists. In an introductory passage Roe tells us that she herself has known the "driving necessity to keep on doing research that is characteristic of all who have experienced its satisfactions," but the need to subordinate her work to the welfare of her family has always exercised the far stronger influence on her, and although she insists she is speaking only for herself, the implications of Roe's words in the extended context of her book is that what is true for her is true for all women at all times in all places.

The social homogeneity, the worship of intellectual accomplishment, the belief that it is in the nature of things that only men may do the work—in 1953 these constituted a set of opinions applied to scientific life that had a long history, and reflected the influence in American education of certain European values and institutions, in particular that of the nineteenth-century German university where bearded men in black frock coats studied in solitude and were dedicated to the idea that the pursuit of knowledge was a holy mission undertaken by few, and succeeded in by even fewer. There were those who lived in the world, and there were those who lived to understand the world: the profound character of the latter could hardly be disputed. Certainly, a life in science belonged to this idea of the university.

I. I. Rabi, the distinguished nuclear physicist, was one of Anne Roe's subjects in 1953. In 1982, at the age of eighty-four, Rabi was still the perfect embodiment of the scientist formed in the early part of this century. We spoke together one day at his apartment near Columbia University. He told me that he had come to science through religion. His parents had been orthodox Jews; he had loved his family, respected and been moved by their devotion to spiritual life. "But when I discovered physics," Rabi said, "I realized it transcended religion. It was the higher truth. It filled me with awe, put me in touch with a sense of original causes. Physics brought me closer to God. That feeling stayed with me throughout my years in science. Whenever one of my students came to me with a scientific project, I asked only one question, 'Will it bring you nearer to God?' They always understood what I meant."

In this same conversation in which Rabi spoke of touching God through physics, he also told me that women were temperamentally unsuited to science. He confided in me that it was a matter of the nervous system. "It's simply different," he said. "It makes it impossible for them to stay with the thing. I'm afraid there's no use quarreling with it, that's the way it is. Women may go into science, and they will do well enough, but they will never do great science."

*   *   *

The shape and texture of the scientific profession has altered considerably since *The Making of a Scientist* was written. Science is no longer a gentleman's profession, and a few thousand women who either did not hear I. I. Rabi telling them they could never be great scientists, or were listening to other voices telling them other things about a life in science, followed compulsions that would not be deflected and entered the profession. The social homogeneity of science has been altogether broken. Consequently, the mix of appetite, ambition, and talent among scientists is more various today than it has been in the past, and for this reason alone a young scientist often seems alien to an older scientist who may not understand the contemporary vocabulary or syntax, and hence may misinterpret behavior or mistake purpose.

But however much the profession may have changed, one characteristic of the scientist's life remains immutable and irreducible—and that is the act of doing research. Those flashes of scientific insight fed into the structured dailiness of laboratory work and kept alive by moments of discovery—that experience is as central for a contemporary scientist as it was for Galileo. It is in the act of doing research that one truly sees what it means, what it has always meant, to be a scientist. Research is the live heart of the scientific life; around it there gathers status, ambition, careerism, and professional values. If research dies for a scientist that life becomes an empty shell, its live substance has been sucked dry. Greatness of position, respect for past accomplishments, the Nobel Prize itself— none of these can compensate for the loss of vitality only research provides. For every human being the present must be won each day anew, and for a scientist it is won only in the laboratory. It is here that a scientist establishes his or her claim on, possession of, organic relation to work, real work.

The research scientists I spoke with provided me with a perspective, focused steadily against a range of personality and motive, which constituted an illumination on the meaning of work. In 1953 Anne Roe set out to discover what kinds of minds scientists had. The question these women raised for me was not, "What kinds of minds do these people have?" but rather, "What does it mean for a thinking mind to be at work?" Inevitably, all responses and elaborations led back to the laboratory.

The scientists' associations to the act of doing research were remarkably reminiscent of how an artist arrives at the act of making art. The analogous condition served me well. It clarified and extended my ability to locate the pleasure and the satisfaction, the urgency and the compulsiveness, to think more clearly about the imaginative source of scientific research, understand better the inner atmosphere in which it grows. It seemed both touching and important that this information was coming to me through women who, as a class of being, are now engaged by an immense act of self-creation. Art, science, feminism: they came to seem metaphors for each other.

The English writer Radclyffe Hall was once vacationing at a small seacoast town. She walked into a hotel dining room, and her eye fell on two women—one forty, the other sixty— sitting together at a table for two. Hall looked at them and thought: Gentle tyrant mother and virgin daughter withering on her stem. Out of that sentence she wrote her novel *The Unlit Lamp,* fulfilling brilliantly the promise of the single compelling thought.

Radclyffe Hall had had a flash of psychological insight as she watched the two women in the hotel dining room. It was the kind of insight that derives from an inner musing, continuously at work inside a writer, on the dynamic of human experience. Partly conscious, partly not, half-awake, half-dreaming, the writer is always wondering: How is it between people, and why? What keeps these two together and pulls these two apart? And what is the relation here, among these three, or these four? Is the connection life giving or death dealing? Is it symbiotic or parasitic? Central or tangential? Vigorous or inert? What is going *on* here? Even when writers don't fully register these thoughts, they are having them. It is how they take in the world, how their knowledge of imaginative life matures, and their art is fashioned.

Scientists do what writers do. They also live with an active interiority, only the ongoing speculation in their heads is about relations in the physical world rather than the psychological one. The natural biologist walks through a city park, across a suburban lawn, past an open shopping mall, and is half-consciously wondering: Why two leaves instead of three? Why pink flowers instead of white? Why does the plant turn this way instead of that way? Such rumination goes on without end in a scientist's mind, a continuous accompaniment to the rhythm of daily life. Whatever a scientist is doing—reading, cooking, talking, playing—science thoughts are always there at the edge of the mind. They are the way the world is taken in; all that is seen is filtered through an everpresent scientific musing.

It is from inside this continuousness of thought and perception that the scientist, like the writer, receives the crucial flash of insight out of which a piece of work is conceived and executed. And the scientist (again like the writer) is *grateful* when the insight comes, because the insight is the necessary catalyst through which the abstract will be made concrete, intuition be given language, language provide specificity, and real work go forward.

Real work consists of testing an idea to see if it proves out: is the notion plausible, are the findings persuasive? In order to test, one must provide a control. For Radclyffe Hall the control was the novel. For the scientist the control is the laboratory experiment. Hall worked out her insight by writing her book and discovering her people as she wrote. Her insight proved out: it yielded up a piece of imaginative reality. If the scientist's experiment proves out, a piece of physical reality is substantiated.

Had Hall's insight not been a true one she would have cried: "It's not working! I can't make it come right. These people aren't at *all* who I thought they were"—and she might have thrown down her effort in despair and consigned her manuscript to the wastebasket. On the other hand—and this is the more likely—she might have said: "It's not turning out as I expected, but isn't this interesting! Look who these people *are* turning out to be, and see where they're taking me" (as Tolstoy said when Anna Karenina persisted in taking the novel away from Count Vronsky). The scientist, when faced with an idea that's not working out, may also allow the sense of failure to prevail and may abandon the insight, or—and again this is the more likely—the failure will be interesting to the scientist, lead to questions not previously thought of, and result in a wholly unexpected piece of work.

The question a scientist asks determines the scope of scientific content. The design of a scientist's experiment is the equivalent of a writer's style. The skill, beauty, and depth with which style and content are joined is, for both scientist and writer, the measure of accomplishment, and both alike are stern in the judgment of fellow workers deemed insufficient in either.

But good or bad, major or minor, asking the largest of questions or the smallest, doing meticulous work or getting results with crude methods, a scientist or a writer is one who ruminates continuously on the nature of physical or imaginative life, experiences repeated relief and excitement when the insight comes, and is endlessly attracted to working out the idea. Excellent, competent, or mediocre, these are people whose most absorbed, alive, and focused hours are spent either writing or doing science—people for whom the work has become addictive: deprive them of it and they suffer acute incompleteness.

There is mystery but also there is meaning. A biochemist remembers that after her first day in undergraduate biology she came home, walked into her neighbor's house, and said, "Do you know why the eggs form little strings when you scramble them?" The neighbor said no, she didn't know, and the future scientist gave her the biochemistry of scrambled eggs. "Do you know," the scientist says today, "tears were standing in my eyes, so great was my happiness at this discovery. It was like revelation. I felt a whole world standing behind the chemistry of scrambled eggs, waiting for me to enter and explore it. I wanted to learn everything there was to know in biology and chemistry. I *had* to learn everything."

Every scientist must experience this moment at least once: without it a lifetime of work in the laboratory cannot be sustained. To some scientists that flash of wholeness comes early, to many it comes late; in some the memory of that moment is strongly alive, in some it flickers more dimly; but the work done every day all over the world, in physics, brain research, and biology, is done because each of the men and the women doing it was once overtaken by a transforming perception of the physical world as whole and knowable.

How a would-be scientist makes substantive his or her relation to the visionary enterprise—decides on a discipline, settles on a problem, and goes to work—is often as much a matter of chance as it is of temperament. One can as easily become an experimental psychologist, or a neuroanatomist, or a chemist because of where one went to school or whose influence one happened to come under as because of a compelling early response to the logic of chemistry or the beauty of the human nervous system. No matter. Once the discipline is established, the problem chosen, and the scientist immersed in the work, he or she becomes as persuaded as need be of the centrality and urgency of the particular work being done. Such adaptive myopia is necessary in science because the grinding, repetitive minuteness of daily laboratory work is so consuming (for weeks, months, even years at a time) that often, even to remember the original impetus for the work is a psychological trick of the highest order. To stimulate the memory back into existence with fair regularity one must believe in the fundamental importance of what one is doing. Those who do are the most energetic, vital, exciting, and excited of scientists.

Carol Steiner, a forty-year-old geneticist at a medical school outside of Philadelphia, comes up with a fine metaphor for how to make a working proposition of scientific mystery. "Imagine," she says, "that you have a jigsaw puzzle with no picture printed on it. All you have is pieces you haven't a clue how to make sense of. The pieces are your separate scientific observations. Here's an example of how you might try to get a handle on the puzzle:

"We have a microorganism with a secretory structure on one end. We know this structure is always on the same place in the cell, and that the position of this structure is inherited. The question that we want to answer is: how can inherited information be translated into positional information? Why in that one place, and no place else? Is the genetic code involved, and if so, how? The answer will tell us how the genes work in concert with the rest of the cell to put things where they belong.

"In order to gather pieces of the jigsaw puzzle (that is, pieces of information), we poke at the cell. We change it a little. Now, there are two ways to change the cell. One way is to mutate away the structure and then hope to find out what has changed biochemically inside this cell so that this structure is no longer made. The other way is to make mutations which

affect known events occurring in the cell, defining these alterations precisely, both genetically and biochemically, and then
ask how these alterations affect the formation of the structure.
In my kind of genetics we do the latter.

"A specific mutation that altered the membrane structure
of the cell was found to turn off the synthesis of the secretory
structure. This was a piece of the jigsaw puzzle. But just one
piece. Because we hadn't a clue as to how this *had* happened
or *could* happen. Then we got another piece of the jigsaw. It
was found that shutting off replication of the chromosome
(DNA synthesis) also shut off the formation of the structure.
Then we found that mutants which shut off membrane synthesis in fact also shut off DNA synthesis, and two pieces of the
puzzle were put together to form a working hypothesis: the
structure synthesis of the secretory structure was shut off by
mutants in membrane synthesis *because* these mutants in membrane synthesis *first* shut off DNA synthesis. This hypothesis
suggests many further questions that will lead to experiments
whose results will print pictures on the pieces of the jigsaw
puzzle. Not put the puzzle together, mind you. But help us
think about what the picture will ultimately look like."

The realized picture on Carol Steiner's jigsaw puzzle is the
map of gene expression laid out clearly with all roads, path-
ways, connecting signal points, and railway junctions marked
out so that any tourist can find his or her way in this beautiful country which is confusing only when one is wandering
about in ignorance—as we all are now—with a highly incom-
plete map.

Steiner is a scientist for whom that flash of scientific wholeness—which came to her through genetics—is recalled regularly. When she speaks of the position of the secretory structures on the cell ("The question we want to answer is why in
that one place, and no place else") her speech is repeatedly
animated by the sentence "This is a question *fundamental* to

developmental genetics." The single piece of information about the position of the secretory structure is what Steiner concentrates on in her daily working life, but worrying it, obsessing over it, learning everything there is to know about it, figuring out what it *really* means inevitably puts the glow back in her mind, makes her remember why she does science.

Another scientist with a strong sense of the relation between developmental genetics, moments of discovery, and the daily work in the lab is Sharlene George, a thirty-five-year-old yeast geneticist (colleague and collaborator of Carol Steiner). With Sharlene one begins to see exactly how a scientist lives with a problem for months and years at a time.

Sharlene George works with Tetrahymena because it is an organism whose cells resemble those of humans more than do the cells of bacteria (a Tetrahymena cell, unlike a bacterial cell, has membranes, structures within the cell, lateral chromosomes). George's genetic interest became the regulatory function of the cell's outer membrane. The question she asked as a graduate student was: How does the cell elaborate and control its membrane?

An experimental approach important to biological research—and the one Sharlene George adopted—is the creation and study of mutations. Thousands of mutants are artificially bred in laboratories and studied by scientists who try to see exactly where and how they differ, and deduce what is happening biologically as a result of the departure from the normal. A cell biologist will commonly take a small "known" in the cell, mutate it, and see what can be deduced about the whole from this one specific.

This was Sharlene George's small known: The membrane is composed of an elaborate "sheet" of lipids and proteins that hang together not out of electrical impulses but out of a kind of affinity and an indissolubleness (beads that don't dissolve out). The question: How does the cell make this complex sheet of membranes? That is, how many genes in the organism have the information for telling the cell to make the different components of the membrane? How many genes encode for a particular function? How many genes regulate that function? How is regulation carried out?

It takes years for a scientist to even begin to answer such a question. Hundreds, literally hundreds of experiments are made by first growing large laboratory cultures of cells, then adding to these cells a mutagenic compound that produces hundreds of random mutations, then screening repeatedly for the mutation that will yield up useful results. After which begins the real work: observing keenly, intently, endlessly the results of these mutation experiments to make both large and small sense of them. What's alike here? What's different? How does this square with the last six papers written on this subject? Where does it fit into the theoretical picture? Does this *change* the theoretical picture?

The work is both tedious and imaginative. One must have the patience to perform the experiments meticulously (if the experiments are not absolutely clean and precise they are useless; above all, a scientist's experiments must be such that they can be replicated). Then one must do many, many, many experiments, over and over and over again, so that a legitimate data base is accumulated. Then one must sit down with the data and think hard about it, sifting through one's mind all the literature, all the conversations, all the odd thoughts one has read and had on the subject.

Sharlene George's Ph.D. dissertation established that many genes controlled the structure of the fatty acids of the membranes. This took three years of work, years in which she designed, executed, and analyzed hundreds of cell mutation experiments in the laboratory. Membrane biogenesis remained her subject. Today she is a highly granted principal investigator running a laboratory filled with technicians, graduate students, and post-doctoral fellows. On the shelf above her desk are five dissertation theses by graduate students who have worked in her laboratory, each one advancing the question, adding information to the large picture of how cell regulation of the membrane works.

Slowly, as the years have gone on, an overriding interest developed in this lab. There were four protein components which appeared to be regulated in a common manner. The people in Sharlene George's lab wanted to know: How does the cell control the relative proportions of these four components?

Hundreds of experiments with mutants have been made here over the last few years by changing the DNA which gives altered enzymes to make one or another of these compounds. The genetic structure of each of the mutants was studied and its biochemistry analyzed. A great deal of information was amassed, many speculations filled many notebooks, many conversations went on well into the night. Nothing really jelled.

"I was always thinking about the problem," says Sharlene. "When I was doing something, nothing, anything. Shopping at the supermarket, talking with my friends, cooking dinner. This question of the proportions of the components was always there, waiting for me. It's as though circuits are forged in the brain after years of work. These thoughts become an accompaniment to the day's activity. They're a comfort when I'm down, a goad when I'm lazy, a prod and a friend.

"It came to me on a Friday night in the shower, when I was getting ready to go out. I suddenly realized that a major factor in controlling the proportions of these components was the cell's response to a single precursor. I saw that the response was mediated through the membrane *itself*. The precursor caused an alteration in the activity of an enzyme in the membrane, and this alteration was transmitted to the cytoplasm and turned off the gene responsible for synthesis of the precursor.

"I ran out of the shower dripping wet and immediately put my conclusions on paper. They really *were* synthesizing! Suddenly I could account for so much that had remained puzzling. I was able to make a table of correspondences that explained a dozen different activities in the membrane and accounted better than anything else for the regulation that had been observed. It was a eureka moment.

"I got so excited I began to tell my husband about it. But I really needed to talk to another scientist. I had to call Carol and tell her. Five years of work, and it had come out so beautifully! It was one of those times you think, Jesus, I've put a tiny piece of the creation in place. I was *flying*."

Carol Steiner confirms the memory of that night. "Do you realize what she had done? She had shown that changing the consistency of the membrane affected what happened inside the cell. This revealed that there's a conversation going on between the membrane on the *outside* of the cell and the genetic machinery *inside* the cell. It's a fundamental observation on one of the ways in which the cell controls its own life processes. It was a fine piece of work, the kind of work that reminds you of what it's all about, and keeps you going for *another* five years."

"But you've got to love it all." Sharlene sighs. "The rote work in the lab, the drudgery, the disappointments, the niggling difficulties that can make you jump out of your skin with impatience. Some days you come in, nothing goes right. The petri dishes aren't clean, the water is contaminated, nothing's growing, the equipment isn't working, the results aren't coming up clean. Everything takes forever. Weeks, months. *Forever.* You gotta love it, anyway. Or else you can't get to the moment that makes it all worthwhile."

Sharlene George's eureka moment was an "easy" triumph; her insight was immediately accepted by her fellow scientists as right and real. But there are scientists for whom the eureka moment comes and goes, and instead of yielding pleasure and victory it yields the pain of anticlimax. The finding is not acknowledged. Other scientists respond with "I do not accept the truth of what you are saying."

Such an occurrence in a researcher's life can create, or reinforce, the obsessiveness for which scientists are famous. Behind many long pieces of research—all requiring patience and intensity, childish stubbornness and the maturity to delay gratification—lies a wounded sense of rightness: "But don't you *see?* It's so clear. How can you not see?" Anna Wulf is a living embodiment of a scientist's driven need to make the opposition "see."

Imagine Eleanor Roosevelt with dead-white hair, eyes that blink rapidly behind thick glasses, and a heavy German accent; softspoken and courteous, the intellectual authority is established immediately she begins speaking of her work. Anna Wulf is a seventy-five-year-old neuroanatomist honored today for the work she did together with her husband, Heinrich Wulf, for more than thirty years—work whose validity was for many of those years denied and repudiated, forcing the Wulfs to sustain intellectual isolation of a high and prolonged order, during which they were shored up only by each other and the stubbornly shared conviction of the rightness of their insight.

Heinrich and Anna were both graduate students at the same institute in Germany in the late twenties. While working on his Ph.D., Heinrich made what he thought was an astonishing discovery: He saw that certain neurons in the hypothalamus contained secretions very similar to those of secreting glands. He also observed that the structure of these neurons, different from that of other neurons, resembled the structure of glands. He then posited that there must be some relation between the peculiar structure of these neurons and the fact that they specialized in secretory activity (this was long before it became a piece of conventional wisdom in science that the relation between function and structure is intimate).

Heinrich's early findings were published in 1928. Anna, a graduate student in the laboratory where Heinrich had carried out his experiments, became excited and persuaded by them. She offered to work with Heinrich on the enormous task of substantiating his brilliant insight. To her amazement their fellow scientists did not immediately see, as she did, that Heinrich's insight was true and important. They were dismissing it as wild, impossible.

Sitting at the desk in her laboratory office more than fifty years later, Anna Wulf explains the problem metaphorically. She points to the telephone on the desk and says, "If this phone were to ring now, it would be because someone is calling me. The message is specific and private. It is meant for me alone. That is how the nerve cell system works. Nerve cells make close contact with other cells to convey specific, directed signals.

"Now imagine a public address system operating in a large room filled with people doing various things. Everyone goes on eating, reading, talking as the message blares out across the hall. But one man who hears his name called jumps up to take the call. That's how a hormone gland system works. Endocrine glands secrete a substance into the blood that is distributed indiscriminately throughout the body and 'reaches' cells that are attuned to them.

"It was steadfastly insisted by our colleagues that these systems are unrelated, and unlinked. It was not possible, they said, that a neuron could do what a gland did. But we had *seen* those neurons. We had seen what they looked like. It was impossible that it meant nothing. It must mean *something* that they looked like glands.

"Well, our colleagues couldn't see what we saw. 'You'll have to show us more convincingly than you have until now.' So we did."

Anna and Heinrich married and worked together for more than thirty years to demonstrate systematically that certain neurons in the brain of almost every creature duplicate the activity of internal glandular secretion. For them, the idea of neurosecretion became both a burden and a source of immense stimulation. That passionate, stubborn, obsessive "We had *seen* those neurons; we knew they must mean something" kept them going through some remarkably discouraging times. They were now identified with their secreting neurons, they had to make the others see what they saw.

Wherever they worked everyone knew that Anna and Heinrich were true collaborators, that their intellectual gifts were complementary, that each one provided an indispensable contribution to the scientific partnership. Yet, for more than twenty-five years Anna Wulf worked without pay and without position in a corner of her husband's laboratory. "You know," she says softly, "the nepotism rules were fierce in those days. And even if they *hadn't* been. Professorships for women were unthinkable. No woman got one, under any conditions, anywhere. If Heinrich had not been determined that we would work together, had not supported me as a scientist, completely and totally, I would never have done anything. There simply would have been no way for me to work. As it was, things were very hard for us, very hard indeed, and for a very long time."

They divided up the animal kingdom between them: He took vertebrates, she took invertebrates. He worked on fish, toads, oppossums. She . . . she's suddenly embarrassed: "Well, you see, there was absolutely no money to spare. We couldn't buy insects for me to work on. So I used to go down into the basement and collect cockroaches. And that's what I worked on for years. Cockroaches. Well, let me tell you, this shameful practice had the most remarkable results. The homely cockroach (many of our assistants refused to touch them) turned out to be a creature whose brain it was a pleasure to dissect and analyze, and it made a very important contribution to our studies."

By 1937 the Wulfs had collected an enormous amount of evidence that a secretory process was going on in certain neurons in the brain. When *this* evidence was dismissed at a conference in Europe filled with the kind of scientists who should have seen what the Wulfs were getting at ("The evidence does not deserve acceptance at this time" was the stiff verdict), Heinrich lost heart. It was Anna who stabilized him and insisted they push on.

Shortly after this conference the Wulfs left Germany for the United States where with one professorship after another, in different parts of the United States—Heinrich Wulf set up a laboratory, and Anna Wulf worked beside him. Year after year after year they performed endless experiments on their various creatures—removing the brain, putting it in a fixative, staining it so its inner structure would be revealed, looking at it under the microscope; or, alternately, removing a gland, looking to see what effect the removal had on the brain, what exactly happened in the body, whether the secretion of a nerve cell was released into the bloodstream in the same way as that of an endocrine gland and therefore could act as a hormone did; and with both sets of experiments, taking scrupulous notes on their observations, thinking hard about how to find yet another way to present their observations, gathering them into an everwidening context of scientific reference and into more and more irrefutable evidence.

By the mid-fifties the truth of what the Wulfs had seen in 1928 was finally understood and acknowledged, and by the early seventies it was celebrated. Their work led to the realization that the brain and the hormone glands work in close collaboration: In order to be "understood" by a gland, the brain uses the "glandular language" of secreting neurons. This interaction between the two central systems governing the body had to be generally understood before neurosecretion could come of age.

Anna Wulf's entire adult life has been spent in the laboratory. To this day she doesn't feel quite right or real outside of the lab. "The laboratory is where you always want to be," she says. "It's the only place where you feel yourself. It's not that you're having miraculous insights, or making great discoveries every day in the lab. But . . . you feel tired or lonely or depressed, or excited or overstimulated, or nervous or very focused—you go to the lab! The lab is home. The lab is where you putter around, or check the equipment, or go over the data, or make a cup of coffee and stare at the experiment. It's the atmosphere in which your mind is working, even when you don't know it. You're in the lab. Something will happen.

"And it's the *only* way it will happen. That thinking machine must be going all the time. If it's not, you simply won't get it. The thing that must happen won't happen. Being a part-time scientist will not work. That's why most women scientists have not been able to do good science. Because they've always been forced to be part-time scientists. But part-time work"—she shakes her head no—"it's like pushing something halfway up a hill. You don't get credit for the fifty percent you tried because that fifty percent won't get you to the top of the hill."

The top of the hill is working out the scientific insight; that, finally, is everything. She is an old woman now. She sits back in her chair in her lab office, folds her hands calmly in her lap, and delivers herself of a piece of wisdom it has taken her a lifetime in science to come to: "The thing about it is, you can't get it with money. Or by pushing people around. Or by having fifty technicians. Either you've *got* the creative insight, or you don't. It's that simple. And if you've got it, you're driven to work it out. And yes, you're driven to make others see it as you see it. You keep working and working and working, because you *know* you're right. And sooner or later they've got to see you're right. Then you can rest. You can go on to something else."

"I know how she feels. The pain of knowing you're right without anybody else understanding where you're coming from is awful, and it's just as she says, it *drives* you. She at least is out of the woods. She's seventy-five years old, she's worked fifty years, she was right, and now they all see she was right. Me, I'm in the middle of it. Every time I do an experiment nobody believes that it's going to turn out the way I say it will. It doesn't always, but most of the time it does. How do I tell people I know what I'm doing? 'Wait and see, it *feels* right'? *Feel* is no good in science. You have to have a theory. And I do. But at this point it's general, and until I get it down into its specifics, I'm left with *feel*. I've been doing experiment after experiment to tie it down. Before each experiment people say, 'It won't work.' And I say, 'Wait and see.' Eventually, I'll be able to put these experiments together and say, 'See? There's a coherent theory here, and the theory makes sense.' "

Lorraine Miller is a forty-two-year-old cognitive psychologist who believes the brain seeks meaning, and that it does so at the simplest, most immediate level of sensory intake. Lorraine has been doing experiments in vision research to demonstrate this thesis for more than fifteen years because: "I don't believe a reductionist view of the mind. I don't believe anything as beautiful, powerful, and inventive as the mind can be described by terms that don't include the kinds of things a mind does, like *symbolize* and *intend*." That classic "I don't believe it" is the necessary heart of her scientist's arrogance.

When Lorraine entered graduate school in 1961, experimental psychology was just beginning to feel the impact of both the new computer technology and Noam Chomsky's work. The people thinking about the mind were linguists like Chomsky, philosophers, neurophysiologists, psychologists, and computer scientists trying to create an "artificial intelligence." Enormous excitement surrounded the field of cognitive psychology, then in its infancy. The expectation prevailed (it still does) that computers could provide a step-by-step model for how the brain actually worked. The idea was exhilarating, given, as Lorraine says, four hundred years of scientific belief that all sciences could be reduced to physics: "Computers were a breakthrough. Cognitive psychology owes its emergence to computers. They not only provided real, concrete ways to test theories of mental processes, and real, concrete examples of 'thinking machines,' but—more important—they removed the philosophical turmoil over whether it was kosher for a scientist to study something she couldn't see. They freed us up to stop worrying over whether it was okay to study mental processes, and just start studying them.

"But old habits of thought are hard to break," she continues. "The models of how we make sense of what we see, which have emerged from this computer work, remain reductionist. Here's a classic example: A leading theory of how visual perception occurs is that there is a sequential set of transformations on an image, beginning with the simple sensory registration of information at the retina. The theory states this information is transformed into simple physical features like color, width, length, and so on, and that these features are then combined to give us the pictures we have in our heads. This was a typical theory handed to us as graduate students."

Lorraine explains why many researchers her age could not accept this explanation for how the visual brain worked: "To begin with, we had just come out of behaviorism, that fifty-year blight on psychology which had said there was no mind at all, so there was rebellion against *that* tradition. And then these were years when many of us felt that science had to change its response to researching the biological and psychological systems, that habits of thought reflexively opposed to the idea of the mental were no longer fruitful.

"So here I was at the sensory end of cognitive psychology— an attempt to figure out how this extraordinary phenomenon, the human visual intelligence, organizes itself—and I was being told a child's tale. *First* there is sensory input, *then* there is transformation of that input into recognizable simple features which are matched against a template in the memory (that is, a collection or list) that identifies single objects, *then* somewhere further up the line all this becomes consciousness.

"I just couldn't accept this. It was an idea that denied context, complexity, constraint. There's so much the brain has to do to make sense of images that it could never accomplish its task if all it had to work with were a couple of rinky-dink features and a list of possible objects. And anyway, it can't *have* a list of possible objects. Every time you go to the movies you see sequences of images you never saw before. How can you understand what's flying before your eyes if all you've got in your head is a list against which to check off possible objects resulting from possible combinations of features? You can't. Something much more intelligent, integrated, *directed,* purposeful is happening in that visual brain to enable you to see five new faces over the credits and recognize every one of them in the next frame.

"Somehow, the brain has to start being intelligent about the sensory input, figuring out the meaning of what is before it *this time,* in this *particular way,* right from the start. How? Nobody knows. But it doesn't just work blind, doing this automatically up to the point of consciousness and then whammo! consciousness, thought, deliberation.

"It seems to me it's a mental 'conspiracy' from the very beginning. Every component of the visual system from the simple ones on up is in on the conspiracy, figuring out where things belong in space and describing what they look like. There is a unity of purpose and function, and it's *mental* from the beginning."

This "feeling" of Lorraine's, that simple sensory mechanisms must begin the symbolic work, the work of visual intelligence (the "mental" process), is what is called a hunch in science rather than an idea deduced from hard evidence (such as Anna and Heinrich Wulf's secretory neurons). A scientist's hunch ends either in glory or in disaster. If the hunch is wrong, twenty years can go down the drain and the scientist will be thought a shabby loser, a wrong-headed person not worthy of the profession's respect. If the hunch is right, the scientist is acclaimed a visionary, a brilliant loner, a person of self-sustaining genius. The scientist in the grip of the hunch can only hope—because the hunch presses on the scientist's heart, will not relinquish its claim on the inner attention, attains the character of a helpless attachment.

Lorraine Miller's hunch that complex symbolic visual activity is part of what "simple" sensory systems do has dominated her life as a scientist for more than fifteen years. It has made her devise experiment after experiment to acquire hard evidence for her thesis, to establish the truth of what she "sees," and to force from her fellow scientists the recognition that she has been right all along in an approach that has often been dismissed as wild, maverick, irresponsible.

In one experiment Lorraine showed that the visual system gets more sensitive to a tiny line segment when it appears in a picture of something, rather than when the segment is presented alone on an empty ground. In fact, Lorraine has shown that the visual system responds twice as fast to the line segment when it is seen in a picture rather than when seen alone. "You might say the line segment in the picture is being treated in a privileged way." Lorraine laughs. Then she leans forward intently. "Now, is this mental?" she asks her visitor. And immediately answers, "The *change* in sensory response is a change due to visual meaning, and it's also a change which furthers the computation of that meaning." She goes on to describe an experiment that will explain better what she is talking about:

"We know from neurophysiology that different nerve cells in the visual cortex are selectively sensitive to different simple physical features—that's what inspired the theory I mentioned earlier that all it takes to perceive something is the simple combination of these physical features. In any case, feature-sensitive nerve cells do exist. One will respond well to a bar of a certain width in a certain orientation, another will respond well to a bar of another width in another orientation. If you stare at an alternating pattern of black and white bars for a minute it is harder for you to see those bars afterward. It's as if all those nerve cells that are specialized to respond to bars of that width and that orientation have grown tired. However, if we show you bars of a different orientation or width, you'll have no trouble seeing them because the nerve cells that are specialized to respond to *those* bars of *that* width and orientation have no reason to have grown tired. Because we psychophysicists don't go probing inside the head to show this—we don't actually measure the nerve cell's activity, just the effects of that activity—we call these width-and-orientation-selective-mechanisms sensory *channels* in the visual system."

Acting on her general hunch, Lorraine said to herself: Maybe we can show a response of these sensory channels not only when the bars are there, but also when the bars *should be* there. She tried out her idea. The results were elating:

"We placed an object in front of a field of alternating black and white bars, as though a segment of the bars was still there but invisible behind the object. We asked the observer to stare at the object. The small patch of bars was no longer seen!

"This was a crucial test, when the patch of bars disappeared, and more exciting to us than I can describe. The patch of bars had disappeared from perception because the nerve cells there had gotten tired, even though the *physical* stimulation for their getting tired wasn't there, just the mental stimulation of knowing that the bars *should be* there.

"But before we could get *too* excited we had to apply some controls. So we did. We flashed the object alone without the bars behind. In this case the patch didn't disappear. We flashed a field of bars with a hole in it instead of an object in front of it. The patch of bars didn't disappear. We flashed bars in a different orientation, or of a different width. The patch of bars didn't disappear. This indicated that it was the sensory channels specific to these particular bars behind that object that were getting tired. These had persisted in responding to the *context,* and had become weary. The nerve cells that got tired and couldn't see the patch of bars were responding to 'should'—a symbolic feature instead of a simple physical one."

While Lorraine was running these experiments she was living in an apartment a few blocks from the lab. She walked back and forth between home and work at odd and numerous hours of the day and evening, alternately experiencing exhilaration and paranoia: Suppose a safe fell out of a window and hit her or she got run over by a truck before the experiment was completed. She began to pray, "Please God, let nothing happen to me until I see how this experiment turns out."

Remembering this time, Lorraine's face becomes urgent. Then she laughs and relaxes. "Look," she explains, "it's not just that I wanted the experiment to turn out, that I wanted to be right. It's like any intellectual with an insight. You think you've got a piece of the truth. You want them to see not only that *you've* got it, but that it *exists*. It increases our understanding, brings us out of chaos, puts us in striking new relation to what we think we know." Lorraine stops talking, falls into a prolonged moment of silence, then adds:

"But you know what it really is? It's that moment when you suddenly see something new in the world. That moment is so beautiful, it's like nothing else. It demands your loyalty. It becomes you, your essence. And if it's not acknowledged, you're sort of being wiped out. Told the thing you are doesn't exist, never did exist. Worse, doesn't matter whether it exists. And that's just not true. It *matters*. More than anything else in the world it matters."

That moment when you suddenly see something new in the world, that moment is like nothing else. Laura Levin nods her head. The chain of recognition lengthens. She knows exactly what Lorraine Miller is talking about.

Laura Levin, a fifty-one-year-old biophysicist, had worked for years on the molecular structure of the special muscle mechanism whereby the clam keeps itself from being easily pried open (a problem that scientists had worked on since the turn of the century). It was known that all muscles consist of two sets of molecular filaments (myosin and actin), and the generalization had been made that all myosin filaments are organized in the same way in all muscles—that is, in layers, one beneath the other.

Laura's work showed that the muscles of bivalve mollusks

have an extraordinary amount of another, long, rod-shaped protein, which is found in most muscles and which forms a small "core" around which the myosin is organized. In the case of the "catch" muscles, the core is immense—and *this* is where the generalization broke down. Her work took her far enough to make her posit that the core somehow affected the myosin on its surface, and controlled the catch mechanism, but exactly *how* it did this she could not figure out. She worked, worried, calculated, and obsessed.

One October she went off to Europe to forget her problem and refresh herself in Paris, the city of her spirit. Among friends, good food, rest, and general delight, she could not stop thinking about her problem. One night, while she was out walking, in the middle of the street, the solution suddenly came to her. She realized that "the myosin in catch muscles is arrayed on the surface of the core in a single layer so that the *whole* of the molecule can be aligned, as it were, with the molecules in the core and this special, *intimate* relation allows a chemical change on the molecules of the surface of the core that locks in the catch mechanism."

Pacing her living room floor, hands locked behind her back, telling the story in rapid, excited sentences, Laura Levin reminds me that her insight has not yet been verified. But at this moment she thinks she has stumbled on the truth of the matter, and the feel of that original moment of discovery is still strong in her. "It may not sound like much to you—the myosin being arrayed in a single layer on the surface of the core—but believe me, it's like one of those moments in analysis when you *see*—clear, whole, alone in beautiful space—the truth of something you've been staring at *un*seeingly for years. Something so simple, so obvious, so transparently apparent! Ah, you know what one of those moments is like, don't you? You know what it makes you feel?"

Abruptly, Laura stops pacing, turns sheepish, peers at me.

"Don't laugh," she warns sternly. Then her voice softens, and she says: "I felt I was born for that moment. To stand there, on that street in Paris in the middle of the night, with this idea at last clarified in my mind. Oh, that clarification! It was as though the idea had come into my head so that one day I would know the incredible joy of that clarification. Nothing else can touch such an experience for me. Let me tell you, there's not an 'I love you' in the world that can touch it. Nothing."

I told the story of Laura Levin and the catch muscle once during a public talk I gave at a Midwestern university. I had been staying with a mathematician and his wife, a pair of transplanted New Yorkers who welcomed me like expatriates welcoming someone from home; fifteen years in the Midwest had made him eccentric, her long-suffering. When we returned to their house after my talk, the mathematician walked the room like a caged animal and shouted at me: "You are romanticizing science with these pretty tales you tell of the magical moment of discovery. That's not the way it is at *all*. Mathematics is hell. Dreary, isolated *sludge*. Men locked up in small rooms for thirty years with a problem on the desk that never gets solved, and if that problem doesn't get solved it doesn't matter one hell of a tinker's damn what *does* get solved. It's misery, sheer misery. The road to mathematics is strewn with broken, twisted, lost lives. You don't understand the half of it. I'll tell you the *real* story on it.

"When I was a graduate student in the early sixties, the math department of my school was one of the best in the country. They used to hold a colloquium on Wednesdays at noon. Only the best mathematicians spoke at this colloquium. They came from all over the country, all over the world. No students, only great teachers. Well, we had a graduate student, Leventhal was his name, who was so brilliant he was given a

Wednesday colloquium. He had just received his degree, and a great job at Stanford. Now, before he went off, he would present his dissertation to the distinguished assemblage.

"The room was packed. In the middle of the room sat the head of the department of this very university (the mathematician pointed at his living room floor). A hayseed. Writing letters, doodling, making sketches, being generally rude throughout Leventhal's talk. When it was over, and everyone was properly awed, this hayseed suddenly said, 'Mr. Leventhal. The fourth line down in your equation. I don't understand it. Would you explain it, please.' Everyone tittered. Two men in blue suits and thick glasses turned around and leered at him. 'Understanding is a function of the intelligence,' one said, 'perhaps?' Leventhal smiled from the lectern. 'No,' the guy from the Midwest insisted. 'Please explain it. I don't understand.' Leventhal explained. The guy from the Midwest immediately poked two holes in the explanation. A buzz went up in the room. Leventhal explained again. This time, three holes in the explanation. The buzz grew louder. Leventhal began to sweat. He puzzled, and he explained again. The man from the Midwest quietly showed that this explanation was not possible at all. The room was in chaos. Leventhal's adviser got up, left the room, walked through the lobby of the building to a public telephone, called Stanford, told them to cancel the job, came back into the room, and publicly deprived Leventhal of his degree.

"Leventhal eventually solved another problem and went on to become a rather distinguished mathematician. But he was a *broken* man. Do you understand? A broken man."

The mathematician's wife—handsome, overweight, depressed—sat staring at her husband, one finger pushing skin up into her temple. Silence. "For this?" Her bleary eyes spoke for her. "Fifteen years in the Midwest for this?"

"Tell me," I said at last. "What constitutes a legitimate or admirable problem in mathematics?"

"One for which there is currently no existent language of explanation," the mathematician replied. "A problem for which a new language must be devised, one that will change the language of mathematics forever."

"In other words," I said, "every mathematician must write *Ulysses* or he's worthless. A competent hack, perhaps, no matter *how* good he is, but certainly nothing more."

"Exactly," the mathematician beamed, his face gray with anxiety.

A week after the mathematician has told me the story of Leventhal I meet a woman at a party in Boston. She is eighty-four years old, a physical chemist who has spent fifty years as a research associate in a teaching hospital. Dressed entirely in black; strong features in an unruined face; thick white hair wrapped in yellowing braids around the top of her head. The voice is bluff, hearty, self-absorbed; it snorts, it scorns, it opinionates, controls the talk entirely, responds to what feeds her monologue, ignores what doesn't; answers questions in a litany perfected forty years ago; a professional character now, a woman who long ago adopted the style and manner of the de-sexed bluestocking.

Ask her what it was like trying to become a scientist sixty years ago and she replies sharply: "Problem? My dear, I *had* no problem. I knew what I wanted to do, and I simply did it. There was no problem at all."

Did marriage and work seem like experiences she had to choose between? "Never thought of marrying," she snorts. "Never met a man as interesting as the work. Most of them puny little fellers with not much to say to a woman with a mind of her own."

How and when did she know she was going to be a scientist? "I *always* knew I'd be a scientist. Always. There was never any question about *that.*"

How was that? the questioner persists. The old woman repeats: "I simply *had* to be a scientist. That's all there was to it. Never could be anything else."

Why exactly was that? Why did you *have* to be a scientist? Back comes a belligerent stare. The question is rephrased: What was it in science you couldn't do without?

The old woman looks up, startled. The face doesn't have time to settle into mannered dismissal. A surprised smile flashes across its composed features. "Thought," she replies quickly. The questioner looks into her eyes, repaying her by listening hard. The old woman throws back her head, her eyes narrow, for an instant her mouth quivers. Her voice, when it comes, is rich and clear with feeling. "To take part in a free-reigning conversation," she says. "Those moments . . . those rare half-hours . . . when suddenly there is a synthesis of the human intelligence . . . and to know every day that it might happen again today. . . . What else is there in life? *That's* what science has given me. That's why I had to be a scientist."

The scientists I knew would have responded with knowing laughter and a kind of angry excitement to the story of Leventhal, but their eyes would have narrowed with the pleasure of instant recognition at the story of the physical chemist. Leventhal and the Wednesday colloquium is a fable, a tale of man's longing to be more like God and less like man. It mythicizes a fierce and transcendent view of doing science, constitutes a Faustian vision shot through with glory and shame, one having little to do with the meaning of work and much to do with the hunger for genius and the fear that that hunger engenders. The chemist, on the other hand, is a scientist who knows that one experiences oneself in the act of doing, that to experience oneself is everything, and the real power of science for the scientist is that it delivers, on an extraordinarily high level, the significant pleasures of engagement.

Listen to a scientist talk about her work; watch her face as she speaks; the dullest of them is transformed as she recalls what the work does for her. I once asked a medical researcher how she became a scientist. Through a childhood love of mathematics, she said, and began to speak of the great beauty of mathematical order and regularity. She explained that in math there were what mathematicians called subroutines, that each of these subroutines analyzed an equation with more perception than the last, took you deeper and deeper into the problem, made you feel you were penetrating to the center of a mystery, going layer after layer into reality. As she spoke, the researcher's ordinarily placid face became radiant. I saw that it was the thought of solving the problem that so excited her. It was thinking about thinking that made her glow. Mathematics itself, the first instrument of such intense mental excitement for her, was inextricably bound up with the delight she took in the existence of her own expressive self.

Consider the origins of Laura Levin's moment of passion, Anna Wulf's long devotion, Lorraine Miller's sustained intensity, Sharlene George's excited concentration. Each of these women has lived a long time with a scientific problem. Her relation to the problem is fluid, intimate. Each day her interior life fits itself anew to the contours of the problem; her mind stretches and turns, extends itself to accommodate the difficulties, moves about, reaches out, becomes more agile and inventive. Each scientist, as she spoke of her work, seemed absorbed, sometimes astonished, by the action of her own mind. For each of these women, science had clearly become the instrument of the articulated self being formed in the act of doing real work, and in each case I felt it was to the nourishment of this live self that the scientist had become addicted.

Science—like art, religion, political theory, or psychoanalysis—is work that holds out the promise of philosophic understanding, excites in us the belief that we can "make sense of it all." Such work strikes the deepest chords of responsiveness. To act on that responsiveness is to achieve expressive life. That expressiveness is compelling. A bureaucrat, a businessman, a quiltmaker, or an electrician may feel satisfied performing a necessary task well, but the work he or she does cannot induce the level of sustained thought necessary to achieve the clarity of inner being which once experienced cannot be done without. In that moment in Paris when Laura Levin realized the myosin in catch muscles is arrayed in a single layer she felt both erotic and safe, existentially safe. She became a human being made expressive through the power of her own thought: the only kind of sentient creature invulnerable to the sadness and terror of life.

Thus, it is for good reason that original discovery is so fiercely prized in science, and a minor tragedy that it has so often degenerated into a tyranny and a dogma, and become an appalling distortion of its own primary usefulness. The hope of original discovery is a catalyst for engagement, but engagement itself is the point. The struggle of the professional scientist is to be in a position to experience herself or himself through the dailiness of the work. That, finally, is what all the hunger, all the competition, the entire glittering massive moneyed science structure is in the service of.

PART TWO

Women in Science: Half In Half Out

IMAGINE then: To have had science in you. To have known yourself gifted with the means of achieving such articulation of mind and spirit, and to have had the thing almost within your grasp. Almost, but not quite.

George Eliot once wrote a friend that he could not imagine what it was like "to have a man's genius locked up inside you and yet have to suffer the slavery of being a girl." What if you have been a woman, and you have had science locked up inside of you? What then? What, until now, has that been like?

A forty-six-year-old physicist had worked for sixteen years at an industrial research laboratory at the level of Senior Scientist (the equivalent of professor at a university). She had always thought The Lab an eminently fair and decent place. "You did your work, you were treated with respect, that was it." True, from time to time, the question of why there were so few women at her level did come up, but each time her colleagues quite reasonably assured her that The Lab wanted to hire women, it was just that so few women went into science, hardly anyone qualified came their way. If ever one did show up (here a hand inevitably waved in her direction), they were quick to take her.

When the women's movement began making trouble, this physicist was asked to look more closely at The Lab's system of employment and advance. To her surprise, she saw that:

"There did seem to be built-in discriminations that weren't so apparent if you didn't know what to look for. For instance, the scientific supporting staff were of two classes, each of which required only a B.S. for employment. One class was that of Senior Technical Assistant—straight technician, a decent enough job from which there was no place to go, but one in which you could remain for the rest of your life if you wanted to. The other class—the Graduate Studies Program—was a job in which people could go on for an M.S., and then take a place somewhere on the ladder leading to Senior Scientist. When we looked closely, we saw that the first class was all women, the second class all men.

"I didn't feel angry at this discovery. It was, I thought, an understandable, unconcious discriminatory practice, one that would be easy to correct. The thing that I couldn't understand, and that did make me angry, was this: My colleagues were all very intelligent men, men whose grasp of scientific complexity was enormous. And yet, here we came and showed them a rather simple social reality, and they didn't seem to know what we were talking about. They remained puzzled and defensive. They went on saying that if women didn't enter science it wasn't their fault, they took whoever came their way who was qualified. When we showed them it wasn't that simple, they continued to balk. Then I began to think the feminists had something, after all."

Science has a vested interest in the idea of the intellectual meritocracy. It is important to scientists to believe that they act rationally, that they do not distort or ignore evidence, that neither their work nor their profession is seriously influenced by politics, ambition, or prejudice.

Such, clearly, cannot be the case. Scientists, like all other people, make decisions on the basis of a shared social reality, are pulled about by convictions rooted in emotional prejudice, act on inherited ideas of what is natural, and are certainly influenced by politics, ambition, and issues of class, sex, and race. But, as they have a strong need to believe they are guided by intellectual objectivity, they have a more difficult time than other kinds of workers do in perceiving themselves as discriminatory.

Thus, the atmosphere in which women in science have been held back, put off, discouraged and demoralized, frozen in position is particularly disturbing because of its defensive denial that what is happening is happening. In business, a woman looks into the eyes of a corporation executive who says openly to her, "We know what you're all about, we've held you off as long as we could, and now you'll have to take us to court to get what you want." In science, a woman looks into the eyes of a man who thinks of himself as decent, fair-minded, above all reasonable, and who says to her, "I really don't know what you're talking about. Surely you're not saying we've discriminated against you."

Although one knows that life for women in science will not be the same in the next forty years as it has been in the last, right now the statistics on women in science bears out the claim that they are half in, half out. Yes, there is change and growth recorded in the statistics, but that growth in real numbers is small and painfully disproportionate. Between 1978 and 1980 employment of women in science and engineering increased over five times faster than employment of men. Despite this growth women represented about 13 percent of all employed scientists and engineers, and in real numbers the total employment for men in scientific/engineering fields was computed at 2,245,300 while for women it was 314,800. The statistical picture for women in science is graphic and sobering.

Bachelor's degrees earned by women in science and engineering have climbed from 22 percent to 37 percent since

1965, and in 1981 one in every four doctoral degrees in science and engineering was awarded a woman. Nevertheless, in the same year the following proportions of female employment in the scientific/engineering fields obtained:

physical scientists	9 percent
mathematical scientists	21 percent
computer scientists	21 percent
environmental scientists	12 percent
engineers	4 percent
life scientists	22 percent
psychologists	35 percent
social scientists	25 percent

bringing women in science to an average of 11.4 percent across all fields.

Concomitantly, the unemployment rate for women scientists and engineers was twice as high as for men in 1980. Doctoral women scientists and engineers were four times as likely as men to be involuntarily unemployed in 1981.

Women in high salaried fields such as engineering, computer science, or chemistry are offered about the same starting salaries as men. However, where demand is low relative to supply, offers to women fall well below offers to men.

The salary differential between men and women widens with age, and is greater at the doctoral level than at the bachelor's level. This is true across all fields of science and engineering. A National Science Foundation graph shows women rising in salary until they reach a 25-year mark of service at which point, on the average, they are making $35,000. Here they level off, and sometimes they even begin dropping. Men, on the other hand, are shown on the graph to continue rising steadily, reaching an average of $45,000 and apparently not falling back at all. Obviously, once women attain the highest grade of employment that is it, whereas men continue to get promotional raises.

Of the people who received Ph.D.s in the 1960s, 62.8 percent of the men are now full professors while 36.5 percent of the women are full professors.

More women pay their own way through graduate school, more men get fellowships and graduate student jobs. Of all graduate students who *do* work, women are much more likely to get teaching assistantships and men research assistantships. It is thought that these facts have implications for looking at dropout rates among graduate students.

It has been said of women in science that they select themselves out. Those words do not sufficiently indicate the experience behind the moment of attrition—the conditions of work under which women in science have felt invisible and discounted, left out and whittled down. Such experience is both subtle and gross; it accumulates from more than one point of origin; is felt as an institutional assault, a psychological infliction, choice forced on one rather than choice freely made. Consider the following:

· An eighty-year-old biologist now being honored for discoveries made in her forties worked for years as a research associate. Another scientist—a man who has known the biologist more than twenty years—was astonished to learn this and said recently, "You mean to tell me she never had a proper job? I didn't know that." It is inconceivable that if the biologist had been a man the scientist would not have known he did not have a proper job.

· A sixty-eight-year-old physiologist active all her life in university research said, "I worked for years among men who never walked into my office to talk to me, who nodded to me in the hall as they nodded to the maintenance men or the cleaning women, never invited me to their conferences or their seminars or their research programs. I was the invisible woman in science."

· A twenty-two-year-old woman who graduated from Harvard in the summer of 1980 with a BS in psychology had entered the university as a chemistry major (she had been an A student in chemistry in high school), but dropped out at the end of the first year: "Freshman chem is taught at Harvard by a famous chemist, a man in his sixties who would put an equation on the board and in a room of five hundred people turn and say, 'Get that, girls?' The first time I heard him say this I laughed. The second time I became angry. The third time I was scared. Something began grinding at my insides every time I walked into that lecture hall. I started thinking, *Do* you get it? *Can* you get it? And then I thought, You *don't* get it. You *can't* get it. I couldn't go on with it. The percentage of boys dropping out of science is high but, believe me, it's a thousand times higher for girls, and I know it's for the same reason I dropped out."

This is the kind of experience that becomes lodged in the psyche: both the individual one and the collective one. It may go unrecorded in the intellect but it is being registered in the nerve and in the spirit. It means sustaining a faint but continuous humiliation that, like low-grade infection, is cumulative in its power and distintegrating in its ultimate effect.

The Research Associate

Ellen Smithing; thirty-seven years old; biophysicist at a Midwestern institute of technology. Born and raised in Iowa, the daughter of schoolteachers one generation removed from farmers, she liked science in high school, graduated from a small women's college as a chemistry major, and went quietly on to graduate school. After she had received her degree, she became a post-doctoral fellow at a medical school in Chicago, and two years later was asked to stay on in the lab as a research associate.

She had never thought of being anything other than a research associate, and was grateful for the offer. "I loved doing science. I loved the systematic nature of lab work, loved physically designing and executing the experiments, even loved washing test tubes and beakers. And I loved thinking about scientific problems, even if the problems were someone else's. Being a research associate seemed perfect. It let me do what I most loved doing.

"I had worked at this lab seven years, and one day I realized I had done the major work on a problem, and I wanted my name first on the paper. The next day I started looking for a job. If not for the women's movement I don't think I'd have realized that my ego needed gratification and that I could get a real job if I tried. I'd still be a research associate."

Sarah Griswold; fifty-six years old; the only tenured woman in the chemistry department of an Ivy League university. She spent twenty-three years as a research associate in this university; eight years ago the feminists on the campus demanded she be tenured; fearful of scandal, the university acceded. Griswold herself has since become an ardent feminist; tenure now is an irony; in the deepest sense she's through with science:

"I came to this university as a graduate student during World War II. When I received my degree there was not the slightest possibility of a woman getting a decent job at a university with research facilities. The only question was, Do you go out to teach at East Jesus Tech, or do you stay on here at this great and benevolent institution as a research associate? For me, the answer was a given.

"To be a research associate was, I thought, marvelous, and I thought so for many, many years. It left me free from meetings, from administrative responsibilities, from having to raise money, or teach classes. I was beyond all that, I could really do research. And the university, I thought, was wonderful. After all, it let me work here, didn't it? It was paying me to do what I loved doing. How could I bitch? What did *I* have to complain about?

"The other side of being a research associate, of course, is that you can never control the laboratory, never set the terms of the work, never be privy to the inner exchanges of the real scientists, never expand, grow, have respect or responsibility.

"I worked here twenty-three years, alongside many men who knew my work was certainly as good as theirs and often superior to theirs. And research associate was all that was ever permitted me. I hate the bastards. They've taken the heart out of science for me."

Margie Clarkson; forty-one years old; a biochemist now working on a trial basis at a research institute in Washington where tenure is dependent on hard work and the publication of research papers. Permanently depressed, her ability to work is severely hampered, and her future as a scientist imperiled.

Clarkson married the most brilliant student in biochemistry at her university when she was nineteen years old, and became a scientist to achieve the comradeship of a working marriage. She had the brains and the motivation; she ploughed through her bachelor's degree and then she ploughed through graduate school. When she received her degree she and her husband went out into academic science as a team—he as professor, she as his research associate. He moved from one excellent job to another, receiving tenure in a series of universities, each one more and more to his liking—better pay, better space, better teaching conditions, better climate, better everything—and

Margie, of course, went along with him, his right-hand woman, always beside him in the lab.

Two years ago her husband announced that he had fallen in love with a graduate student and he wanted a divorce. Clarkson's eyes glaze over, her face petrifies, her voice wanders as she recalls this time: "I never knew what hit me. One day I had everything anyone needed for a decent life, the next day I was wandering around in a state of total disaster. It wasn't just that I'd lost my husband and my home and my job, it was as though I'd lost my place in the world. Not only had I been a research associate all these years—and suddenly I saw it for the dead-end job that it is—but I'd been *his* research associate. I looked around and saw that people I'd worked with for years didn't really believe I could do the work. They thought I'd been riding on his coattails all these years, that I couldn't pull my weight in a lab at all. It was unbelievable. They were making excuses not to give me a recommendation for another job. How I landed this job I'll never know. And to tell you the truth I don't think I'll be able to keep it . . . I'm so depressed . . . I can't shake it . . . I feel like I'm staring into space half the time."

Glenda Pennell; thirty-four years old; a plant biologist who has just been offered tenure at three first-rank universities. She has not yet decided which one she will grace with her political currency as well as her brains. A self-conscious feminist, Glenda feels she must take this factor into consideration when making her choice.

"Yale made me a feminist. Yale and the question of being a research associate. I was always very good at science, very smart, very serious. It's true, like most women, I don't remember thinking too much about my career, about what it meant, or what it took, to be a scientist. I just enjoyed doing science, that's all, I didn't really think beyond that. As an undergraduate at MIT I was the student of a Famous Man. He was my mentor, and he wanted me to do well, and I sort of knew I'd gained entrée to the elite in science through him.

"So I get to Yale and I'm all set, I think. That's day one. On day two I'm shot down. At a separate meeting for women graduate students, the graduate adviser said to us, actually *said* to us: 'You are being trained to become research associates, and to become the wives of the men you are now going to school with.' Mind you, this is 1968. It was devastating. After that not one woman in that class thought of actually going out to get a job.

"I worked in a lab at Yale; we were fourteen women on that floor, grad students, post-docs, research associates. We all knew we had more in common as women working in science than we did as either post-docs or associates or students. Then something crazy happened.

"You know, most scientists have in mind three categories of people when they think of scientists: idea people, technique people, and people who work hard. They think women fall into the last category most frequently, if not always. No one expects a brilliant new idea or technique to come from a woman. Well, one of the women on our floor, a research associate, did something fantastic. She invented a new technique. She'd been doing fine work for years as an associate but now, overnight, she got twelve job offers. Imagine, one day nothing, the next day twelve job offers. That was it. The day after that we were all organizing ourselves to get jobs. For me, of course, it was fairly easy. The minute I had my degree the Famous Man at MIT joined the Famous Man at Yale who now had a vested interest in my future, and I was on my way.

"But that memory of Yale and the research associates has never left me, and I'm not sure where we'd all be today if it weren't for the women's movement. As it is, many of those fourteen women are still either research associates, or they've left science altogether. One of them, Louise Anderson, was a research associate for her husband for sixteen years. She thought hers was the perfect working life. Then another associate, a woman much older than herself, said to her, 'There'll come a time, you'll want to do certain things, and you won't be able to, and then you'll start going backward, there's no way to stop it,' and suddenly Louise realized how restless she was. From there to resentful was one short step. She left Yale, her husband, and science within a year."

Patricia Moran; sixty-one years old; biochemist; tenured professor at the teaching hospital of a large and prestigious medical school in the Midwest. Married thirty years to a professor of surgical medicine, she came to work at the school because they wanted her husband, and they promised him they'd "do something for Patty."

She received a Ph.D. from Yale in 1943 and, "Well, the boys in my class (in those days we were all boys and girls) got twenty-five interviews, I got three. Two of the three were lousy, the third was at Cornell Medical School. It was lousy, too, but it was Cornell. Good people all around, exciting atmosphere, a chance for research. They wouldn't give me a job in the biochemistry department. No woman had ever gotten a job in that department in any medical school. The men just wouldn't have them. You were always used in the departments of medicine where a Ph.D. is inferior to an M.D. They needed biochemists in medicine, of course, but no man would take the job, only women. I worked there as an assistant professor for five years with no hope at all of getting tenure.

"Then I got married and went to Philadelphia with my husband. That's what you did in those days: he went, I went. We came here when he got his job at this school. I became an associate in biochemistry attached to medicine. I remained just that for seventeen years. No money, no sabbaticals, no security, no recognition, and of course no hope of ever getting on a tenured track line. My boss, who was a sweet kindly guy, said to me when I grumbled, 'Patty, you shouldn't be ambitious for yourself. You should be interested in furthering Bob's career.' And when I realized I *was* ambitious for myself I felt guilty.

"My husband left this school for another one in the city twelve years ago. Suddenly, I felt free to act as I wanted to. I went to the biochemistry department and demanded a tenure track position. It was the late sixties. I got it. They made me assistant professor. So there I was, seventeen years after I'd left Cornell, right back where I started.

"I continued working here, getting a renewal of my contract each year, working in my lab. In 1976 I didn't get a renewal in the mail. I called the secretary of the university. It had always been a man. Now the name read L. Cheney. I asked to speak to Mr. Cheney. I was told Cheney was a woman. I said what was on my mind. They said, 'Ms. Cheney will call you back later.' That was at nine in the morning. She called at three in the afternoon. I thought I'd been fired. She apologized for taking so long. I said, 'Don't apologize, just tell me what's happening.' 'You've got tenure,' she said. 'What?' I said. 'That's right,' she said. She said she remembered my saying at some meeting where I was shooting off my damn fool mouth that I was the oldest nontenured professor at the school. She looked into it. It seemed they couldn't keep me this long without giving me tenure. I had it. 'They'll never believe me,' I said. 'Oh yes they will,' she said, 'because I'm the one who tells them when someone's got tenure and when someone doesn't.'

"So, finally, I had it. Not because they gave it to me but because a strong-minded woman discovered it was mine by default."

Academic science is the model for professional science. To rise in this system, one must climb an extraordinarily narrow ladder: from graduate student to post-doctoral fellow to research associate to assistant professor (or principal investigator). The majority of women in science have never completed that rise. They have remained research associates attached to the principal investigator for most or all of their working lives. The cause of arrest is multiple and it has a history.

In an article called "Women's Work in Science, 1880–1910" (adapted from her larger work, *Women Scientists in America*) Margaret Rossiter describes how women began to be employed in the 1880s as assistants in astronomy labs by such liberal academics as Edward Pickering, director of the Harvard College Observatory. Rossiter goes on to observe that "If Pickering and some other observatory directors were progressive in greatly expanding women's employment in astronomy in the 1880s and 1890s, they were not so far ahead of their time as to promote them for important or even outstanding work. Not only did the women have no chance for advancement, they rarely received a raise—at least at Harvard—even after years of devoted service. Because they were not promoted . . . when their scientific work was good, as happened to the more talented men, the female assistants were forced (or expected) to make a whole career out of a job that should have been just a stepping stone to more challenging and prestigious roles."

Here we have a precise truth about women in science—that they've been "allowed" into science for a hundred years now, but for the most part under severely circumscribed conditions, doing segregated work known in the subtext as "women's work." These are the historic beginnings of the woman scientist as permanent research associate.

Women like Patricia Moran or Sarah Griswold (that is, women now in their late fifties or sixties or seventies) could do no other than become and remain research associates, women so hungry to work in science they would accept whatever was permitted them because it was either that or nothing, either here or nowhere, either this sort of today or absolutely no tomorrow. That so many of them did excellent, even brilliant, work is an astonishment.

The male scientist equipped with an ordinary degree of intellectual competence and emotional drive accepts as a given that he is expected to do independent work, not that he will be greeted with amazement should independence surface in his work. Women in science have always had to face the amazement. That amazement is crippling. A forty-eight-year-old research associate explains why:

"The men in science who confide in you, 'The women really don't want the responsibility. I told my associate, do this piece of work with me, we'll put your name on the paper first, and you'll go out and get a job, and she refused, said she liked it just fine where she was.' The stupid sonofabitch. Ask him if *he* lived surrounded by the expectation of failure if he wouldn't be scared to go out there. It's a matter of nerve, and the way I see it, nerve is gathered up in a man no matter how terrified he is, and dissipated in a woman no matter how hungry she is."

It took a scientist of extraordinary, rather than ordinary, drive to do good work as a research associate—someone who could abstract mightily, turn inward, concentrate with a self-sustaining force rare in men and women alike. But there have been associates—starting with those astronomy assistants of the 1880s—who did just that. They were people, these women now in their sixties and seventies, made in a different psychological proportion—the brilliant exceptions in whom the fear of freakishness became a badge of wounded honor, the mind a secret weapon: "The world be damned, I'll occupy a society of one, and I'll think." These were the research associates of forty years ago and more.

Generations of women scientists have been and continue to be made into permanent research associates through marriage to other scientists. Typically, a pair of scientists meet in graduate school, fall in love, and marry. What a romantic couple! Love *and* science. Marriage *and* work. Together in the lab all day, discussing the work at home in the evening. What could be better?

Even if they should get their degrees at the same university and complete comparable post-docs, it has been most usual that he has been offered a job as assistant professor, and she has then "looked around for something in science." That something in science is inevitably a research associateship in or near the university he will be working at; sometimes it is as *his* research associate. It is not at all rare that twenty years pass like a ball moving fast through the air, and suddenly there they are, immobilized in middle life, he full professor and respected scientist, she still research associate.

And then there is the research associate in thrall to the Ivy League, to that conviction bred into all of us, as empire is bred into colonials, that the Ivy League is incomparable, that to be within its walls is to reside inside the Kingdom of Intellectual Heaven, to be outside is to be thrust from Paradise, hurled into an outer darkness where all knowledge and all experience is of an inferior cast.

Sarah Griswold cannot articulate it even now, but one can feel in her that configuration of awe and soul-belief in the superiority of the Ivy League; that in the life and thought interlaced inside these Jude-denying stone walls, was to be found the Kingdom of Transcendent Truth and Beauty—the Great, the True, the Real Science—and that it would be agony for her to tear herself from it. She could not bear to leave The

University—where no woman, whatever the level of her accomplishment, would ever, on the longest day of her life, be made professor.

This historic relation between women, associateships, and the Ivy League is now, prophetically, beginning to alter. In this matter at least the future cannot repeat the past.

A forty-two-year-old physiobiologist, now tenured at a Midwestern state university but with past experience of the Ivy League, says: "When I left a research associateship at the University of Pennsylvania for a professorship in the Midwest everyone in Philly said to me, 'Are you crazy? You're leaving Penn for the Midwest?' I said, 'No, I'm leaving an associateship for a real job.' They didn't get it."

A thirty-six-year-old biophysicist at a Southwestern state university says, "I'd rather be a professor out in the boondocks than a research associate at Harvard. For god's sake, isn't it obvious? To occupy a place on the margin, no matter how great the university, is to give up your life. Now that women are refusing to do that, you'll see how many 'brilliant' women scientists will 'suddenly' emerge in the next generation. You just watch. Because, at the very least, that's what it takes to be 'brilliant,' you know. Not accepting their terms. Risking loss, defeat, and obscurity as they define it."

Five generations of women were willing to occupy peripheral, often humiliating positions in order to do science, and because they were, thousands of young women are now walking through the doors of professional science on the strength of the intellectual legacy the research associates have accumulated. The men who denied many of these women, who would not acknowledge them until they were forced to, nevertheless *knew* the quality of their work, their scientific intelligence, their devotion and their tenacity; knew, as Margaret Rossiter says, that "science benefited from this practice, since the women, having no alternatives, remained on the job for decades and completed many major projects."

Still, the sex-linked connection to the research associate is far from broken. In the late spring of 1980 I walked one evening along the lakefront in Chicago with a twenty-nine-year-old cell biologist. Tall, handsome, with the rangy self-confidence of the American golden girl, Linda Dolan had studied biology under a scientist who had himself not taken the conventional route, suffered for it, not risen in academic science, and proceeded to push her forward because she had become his daughter-surrogate in science. He was convinced that if she made all the right decisions she would be a fine scientist.

A few years ago Linda met another biologist at Woods Hole, married him, and moved to Chicago to be with her husband. Her mentor had urged her to get a university job of her own, but Linda could not find one and "still be married to Ronald." So she had done the next best thing: gotten a fellowship and gone to work in someone else's lab in Chicago. Now, two years later, her husband was unhappy at his job, and they decided to leave Chicago and find a place in the world suitable for them both.

I saw Linda Dolan again in the late summer of that year. She and her husband were leaving Chicago within the month. Ronald had been offered three tenured jobs. At two of the three universities, Linda had been offered research associateships. They had decided on one.

It was a filthy hot afternoon when we walked again on the lakefront. Linda did not look like the golden girl she had seemed in the spring; her good looks seemed abruptly, prematurely faded, without the high color of our previous meeting, her lustrous brown hair dull and lank, her arms white and too fleshy. She knew that I understood the meaning of the historic road she and her husband were about to travel. "Don't worry," she pleaded with me. "I won't do it for long. If something doesn't give, if I don't get a decent job there, I'll leave. I know the danger I'm in."

The Professional Marriage: Four Physicists

Science is strongly marked by professional marriages. Many of these marriages originate in graduate school—either a pair of students fall in love or a graduate student and her professor fall in love—and many of them come out of having worked together—men and women spend long hours in the lab, the intensity of the work is eroticizing, sexual affairs explode easily, and often people fall in love and marry.

Women in science who are married are most often married to other scientists, and consider themselves one half of a professional marriage. The professional marriage does not, cannot mean to the husband-scientist what it must mean to the wife-scientist. He may not even consider himself a partner in a professional marriage; she must. It is possible that neither his intellectual life nor his career will be affected by his attachment to his wife; hers is always affected by her attachment to her husband.

If a husband and wife work together in science, it is almost invariably assumed that he does the "real" work (that is, the thinking), and she the subordinate work (execution of the experiments). Concomitantly, the woman scientist has social access, and obligation, to scientists who mainly associate with her because she is her husband's wife. Thus, she is often in the dreadful position of being scorned intellectually for seeming to receive unearned privilege—a bind from which she cannot readily extricate herself.

If a husband and wife pair of scientists do not work together, then they are faced with the monumental problem of how to live equitably without the sacrifice of either one of their working lives. If husband and wife are friends the worldly circumstance in which these people find themselves is at best difficult, at worst defeating; either way solace and comradeship is required. If they are *not* friends the circumstance of their lives can be brutalizing and may leave one or both with the taste of ashes.

Nina and Leon Braverman are both fifty-three years old: two small, compact people whose faces appear fragile and luminous—as though an intelligence of the spirit is shared between them; they seem to have the same voice as well—gentle, sadly civilized. These two have known each other since childhood. They grew up in the same orthodox Jewish neighborhood in Detroit, discovered their love of science and each other in high school, got married in college, became physics majors, and went on to graduate school together. Leon studied general relativity, Nina high energy physics.

Nina and Leon are Talmudists of physics. Although they have raised three children and live a life apparently indistinguishable from that of most academics, their mutual love of physics is the binding material in a shared inner life that is remarkable for its rigor, its endurance, its primacy. They have spent years meshing their separate intellectual talents for the exquisite pleasure of contemplating physics problems together. For them, physics remained visionary, an exploration to which one gave oneself with a sense of privilege. These are two who recoil from their younger fellow scientists. Nina says of physics today: "There's not a whole person in sight. These people are all careerists manufacturing data."

Nina never cared much about the career, she says, but "Deprive me of doing physics and I start to die." She has had to be more reflective about the matter of being deprived of physics than has Leon. Thinking back on her life in science she says:

"In graduate school I had entrée to a good study group because I was 'one of the boys.' We would get together, a bunch of us, and we'd do the problems. If you weren't able to do that you'd get slaughtered in class. I'd never have survived without that study group. Only years later did I realize that no girls were permitted into the group, and that if I hadn't been Leon's wife I'd never have been in. But being his wife sort of de-sexed me, made me kosher."

Nina's was the fashionable field of physics when they graduated, but it was Leon who got hired at a university three hundred and fifty miles from home. She got a research associateship. After that it was one associateship, or fellowship, or off-the-line grant after another for her. And then, of course, she gave birth to and cared for two children.

Nina sits talking quietly at the wooden table in the kitchen of a shabby frame house in the small Western university town where they have finally come to rest with tenure for each of them: "Leon had one very important insight very early on. He said to me, 'Nina, if you want to be a person like everybody else, you've got to have a regular job.' He was no feminist. Who was in those days? But he saw *that*.

"But we couldn't swing it. For years we tried. Twenty years at least. Leon would keep leaving one job after another in the hope that we'd get me a job also. Impossible. Nepotism rules were fierce, we never seemed to have the pull, or the luck, or whatever it took. But we never stopped doing physics together. Sometimes we worked openly—I'd get a grant and I could apply it to Leon's work, or he'd make his work match the demands of my grant. Something, anything. If not, we'd work on our own, at home, late at night, after we'd done everything else we had to do. The important thing was that I never stopped doing physics. I couldn't. I really felt I couldn't live without doing physics. For years I felt that way.

"Now I can't say that's so true anymore. I'm tired these days. It's odd, but I think my becoming a conscious feminist had something to do with my getting so tired I couldn't work so well anymore.

"We used to go to Aspen every summer. It was an exciting community of people who gathered there, purely for the love of doing science. One summer in the early seventies I was teased about women's lib. I laughed. I'd never thought of women's lib. But I found myself defensive, which surprised me. And in trying to form my argument to defend the women's movement position, I found myself thinking about a lot of things I'd never consciously thought of before. I guess I was becoming a feminist right then and there. Well, we had all been this intimate community of scientists. Now, men I had known a long time suddenly turned ugly. One physicist became exasperated and said to me, 'Listen, women are good for only one thing, having their behinds pinched.' I was stunned. This from a man who'd known me for years.

"After that Leon and I decided we were going to get me a job or go to court. And that's what finally happened. We got these jobs here, with tenure for him when we came, and the firm promise of tenure for me in five years. When the five years were up they denied me tenure, and we sued. It was such a long fight. And it wasn't the physicists who got me tenure, it was the feminists. As I said, I'm tired now."

Forty-nine years old; strong-featured face, brooding eyes, a mass of sexy dark hair she tosses about like a forties movie vamp, the walk seductive and knowing, the mouth sullen and grievance-collecting in repose, then surprisingly girlish in laughter when the eyes fill with a sudden shimmering light. Alma Norovsky is a theoretical physicist at a university renowned for its devotion to the life of the mind. Of her colleagues Alma says drily: "They're very theoretical. People are always asking me how women are treated here. 'Women?' I answer. 'They're a theoretical concept.' "

Divorced four years from the physicist husband she married in graduate school, on her own for the first time in her life, in love with her new independence and happy to be working here, Alma nevertheless sighs. "How do you work in physics, or live among academic liberal men, and not explode all day long every day? Once in a while I'm able to control myself. . . . Last year at a conference I was standing with a group of physicists, all men, and I was introduced to a new member of the group. He said, 'You're the first good-looking physicist I've ever met.' I casually indicated the man standing beside me and said, 'Oh, that's not true. You know Richard here. He's good-looking, and he's a physicist.' They all looked startled, and then some of them nodded their heads appreciatively. I was proud of myself then, but usually it's awful. Still. Always. At every dinner table, in the office, the constant little indications that you don't really exist. You've got to remind them that you're a thinking, working being just like themselves all the time. It's wearing."

She was a pretty girl, bold and flirtatious, loved exercising her power to attract, she'd be damned if she'd give that up ("Why? What for? It was so much fun"). So nobody took her seriously although she was a fine physics student from high school on. Her father, a frustrated scientist, adored and encouraged her, but he floundered. She went to a small women's college where the science courses were bad and the teachers worse, but sexual success made her stubborn and determined on her own seriousness. She bulled her way through into an Ivy League education.

In her second year in graduate school she met and married Lawrence Norovsky, a strongly ambitious fellow student in physics. She says of this time: "I enjoyed being one of the few women in physics, but I certainly did not enjoy it when I realized women in physics were considered ugly, undesirable, clumsy eccentrics. I wanted to be sexually lovely and desirable, and still be a fine physicist." What she doesn't say—although it's apparent—is that she also wanted to attract the attention of a man of power, the kind of man whose interest in her would always be mixed: compelled and antagonistic, attracted by her brains but enjoying her subordinate status as his wife, his relationship to her over the years intermittently eroticized by her professional intelligence, but his sense of her life as equal to his own never maturing.

When Lawrence accepted a job at a university in northern Massachusetts, Alma had had a baby and had not yet finished her degree. She remembers that everyone seemed to be patting her on the head, as though indulging a child's whimsical insistence, when she said she would finish her degree in Massachusetts. But "There were four women in science at the university in Massachusetts. When I think back on it, how those women influenced my life! They arrived one day, sat down in my living room and began giving me full instructions in how to organize myself, my time, my babysitter problem, my shopping and laundry problems. They never for a moment assumed that I wouldn't finish the degree. They had come as compatriots, in a situation they knew nobody but themselves understood, to give me the benefit of their experience. And I did as they said, and finally I finished. But not with any help from my husband, I can assure you.

"When I was just beginning to write the dissertation, and it was in its earliest stages, Lawrence suddenly decided to go to the Physics Institute in Paris for two years. He said to me, 'You can finish in two years. What's the difference?' Then I put my foot down. I don't know why it was, but I suddenly said no, absolutely no, this I will not do. He sent all his friends to see me, to persuade me to go with him. They said I was ruining his career, how could I be so selfish, so I'd finish in a year or two, what was the big deal? I didn't answer any of them, but I stayed where I was. He went to Paris, I sent the children to my parents, and I worked furiously at finishing my degree. Which I did in one year. Then I collected the children and followed him to Paris. Where I was immediately given an office, lab space, treated like a scientist. And the first thing my husband announced was that I was not welcome to join his group for lunch, or anything else for that matter. That was the first time he told me that under no circumstances would we ever work together, that physics was competitive, and he wouldn't have his marriage disfigured by a competitive relationship forming between us. Hah! His idea of avoiding competition between us was for me never to become anything.

"We came back home. Lawrence went to work at Brookhaven. I had three children. I didn't really want to work as a full-time physicist. I got an associateship at Stony Brook. I never was an equal of my husband's physics friends, but I never thought there was anything wrong with that. After all, they worked hard and long, and what was I doing? Why should they treat me as an equal?

"In 1971 I lost my job at Stony Brook, and I couldn't find another one. Suddenly, I was walking around in a daze. What had happened? I'd been a good physicist. I had wanted to do important work. What was I? Nothing. How had I ended up here? What had gone wrong with my career?

"That summer I talked with Nina Braverman at Aspen. We compared notes. It was astonishing how similar the pattern of our lives had been! For the first time it hit me that my life had developed as it had because I was a woman, and I'd made women's choices, and ended up where women in science end up. It hit me like a ton of bricks. All at once, I saw everything. From that moment on I became a rabid feminist. And I mean rabid. Shortly after that my marriage fell apart.

"I remember thinking back to one incident. After I'd lost my job at Stony Brook I was going crazy sitting home, not doing any science at all. One day I was visiting my husband at the lab. Another scientist there, a friend of ours, suddenly said to me, 'Alma, I've got an extra desk in my office. Why don't you come and use it as a guest worker?' That meant no pay but the privilege of working in the lab, using its facilities, and talking with the scientists. I responded gratefully and went to work there. Afterward, I thought, Why is it Lawrence never thought of this for me? How come a friend saved me but my husband never thought of doing so?

"Lawrence was insecure and that insecurity always made him more aware of protecting himself than of seeing his behavior toward me as unjust. And then there was the related, deeper truth that he never took me seriously as a physicist. Why should he when it was so much more convenient not to? He wasn't like Leon Braverman, and if I didn't do it for myself he certainly wasn't going to do it for me.

"I'm sure I'm being unfair to him, and if he were here he'd put a whole different construction on these same events. But that's the reality, isn't it? It's not a matter of fair, it's what we all did to each other, and no amount of looking at it fairly will make me feel any better about my marriage or my husband or the lost working years of my life."

"What Makes You Think You're Worth Educating?"

Margie Clarkson said that two conversations from her school years, placed back to back, were memorable. When she was graduated from college a teacher told her that the most significant thing she had done was to marry her husband.

Then, when she entered graduate school in 1962, the graduate adviser said to her: "What makes you think you're worth educating? You're a woman, and you're already married."

She remembers: "The first time I wasn't insulted. The second time I was. My parents had always acted as though every person was worth educating. Now I was being told I wasn't a person."

Claire Morrissey, a forty-year-old tenured molecular biologist at the N.I.H. had been the first woman graduate student of a Nobel Prize winner famous for his womanizing as well as for his sex-blind encouragement of anyone he feels has scientific fire in the belly. This is how she came to work for him:

"I grew up and went to school in the Midwest. I was good at science in high school and I enjoyed the attention it brought me. It was fun being good at something girls weren't supposed to be good at, but I had no scientific ambition to speak of.

"My college was run on a work-study program and in my second year I went to work in a genetics lab at M.I.T. The structure of DNA had recently been discovered and the lab was filled with the excitement of making scientific history. Everyone knew what they were doing there would fill the textbooks in twenty years. I worked as a technician. The head of the lab thought I was good and told me so. I went back a second summer to that lab. Then the third summer I went to work in the lab of the Nobel laureate. He insisted I come back and take a Ph.D. in his department.

"I didn't know what I wanted to do. I went home and actually it was that summer in a lab in my home city that I devised an experiment, it worked, and suddenly I saw the difference between being the researcher and being the technician. I called the laureate and asked if I could be admitted to his department in September.

"He arranged immediately for me to become the student of

another biologist in the department. But on my first interview with him this biologist said, 'And what are you going to do with your education when you get married and have three children?' I was amazed to find myself offended to the core. In that moment I realized I was serious about science. I turned and walked out the door. And that's how I became the laureate's first, but certainly not his last, woman graduate student."

Millie Warnickey is a forty-two-year-old physiological psychologist working at a research foundation attached to an Ivy League university. A large, bouncy woman, Millie's style is madcap, buoyant, shrewdly self-knowing, carefully reckless. The most highly rewarded, promoted, and fully granted scientist at her foundation, she's all cheerful cunning and good-hearted calculation. Political to the bone, Millie says, "The worst thing about discrimination is having to be cheerful about it." A typically successful Ivy League feminist, she is a master strategist always working hard to get what she wants without alienation or revolution.

Millie grew up in the West, the daughter of a pair of working-class descendants of the pioneers, who taught her to value her own independence. She went to a small college in the Midwest where her untutored love of science was cultivated and nourished. Her favorite teacher had himself been the student of a famous scientist, and spoke often of the Great Man. Millie determined to become the student of this scientist, and when the time came she applied for admission to the university where he taught, was admitted, and presented herself at his laboratory door. The Great Man told her that under no condition would he ever take her as his student because a woman is inherently an inferior scientist.

"I went back to the dorm, lay down on my bed, and to my everlasting shame cried my eyes out. Another grad student—

a man, older than me—passed my door and asked what I was crying about. I told him. He said, 'Come with me.' He took me down to the Great Man's lab and taught me the technique he was famous for. The next morning when The Man came in I was doing an experiment using his technique. He was impressed, and agreed to take me on.

"But what has he learned about women as scientists? Nothing. He considers me a freak, an extraordinary exception, and to this day he will tell everyone he knows that there is only one woman who works like a man in the lab. That is, only one woman who is a real scientist."

Sharlene George, the thirty-five-year-old geneticist at the Philadelphia medical school, is a woman in whom a rage to prevail cohered early. Sharlene had thought she would like to become a doctor. Her college adviser said, "Miss George, in order to get into medical school you'll have to be holier than God." Sharlene's response: "I'll be holier than God." But she found the company of pre-med students distasteful, thought them crude and philistine, bent on money and prestige. In her third year she went to work in a biology lab and decided on research.

By the time she was graduating Sharlene knew that being a woman was a definite disadvantage in science. Wherever she turned at school people seemed continually to be asking, with sharpness and suspicion, if she planned to marry—in which case she clearly would not be fitted for the life of a research scientist. "It seemed as though the only way I could become a scientist was to take a vow of lifetime celibacy."

She had done exceptionally well in school—straight *A*s, all 99th percentiles on her Graduate Record Exam, and had published research as an undergraduate. She applied to a number of fine schools for admission as a graduate student, among them Stanford.

There is a famous Harvard-M.I.T.-Stanford "shunt." It is *the* elite graduate education in science—the assurance of a brilliant career. Students are carefully chosen, and then teachers have a very special interest in educating, grooming, and placing these students during the crucial formative period in their careers. They will become part of an invaluable "old boy network" that has to do with being privy to important work done before publication, special conferences and symposia attended and participated in, elite jobs offered and received.

You must be invited to apply to some of these schools. Sharlene submitted her records and was then invited to apply. She was flown to the interview at the school's expense and underwent eight hours of interviewing with every person of importance in the biology department. She remembers that although many questions were asked about science and her special interests, there were also an incredible number of questions about her plans as a woman. Did she intend to marry? Or to have children? Was she engaged? What was that ring on her finger?

At the culminating session she was interviewed by the head of the department who was, at the moment, a star: "he had recently reported a breakthrough in cancer research, TV cameras everywhere, the phones ringing; he's playing the political, ambitious scientist, hardly speaking to me at all during the interview." When he did speak to her it was to say, "Miss George, do you know why I'm interviewing you?" Sharlene replied that she presumed it was because her records were superlative and she was so clearly a fine candidate for graduate school. "No," the star said. "That's not why at all. It's because this year (it was 1967, the height of the Vietnam War) I'm reduced to the lame, the halt, the blind, and the women."

Sharlene was accepted at this school. She chose to go elsewhere.

*   *   *

Maureen Shaw, a forty-three-year-old M.D. and biophysicist, sits on the admissions committee of the medical school where she teaches. The men on this committee always asked of a woman applicant, "Why should we give you this precious space when everyone knows you're going to take ten years off to raise children?" Shaw says: "I told them, just two years ago, they had to stop asking this question. That it was unfair, irrelevant, illegal, and cruel. But they wouldn't stop. Finally, I told them if they did not stop asking this question of women applicants, I was going to start asking male applicants why they should be considered when everyone knew they were going to die ten years earlier."

Women in Chemistry: Like Jews in Czarist Russia

When I would ask if there was a woman in the chemistry department the answer would often be: "Yes, of course. Haven't you met our Mrs. Godbless? Wonderful woman. She's been with us for years." Mrs. Godbless invariably proved to be a faculty wife who was employed by the year as an associate or a fellow or a visiting professor, and had been teaching freshman chemistry for twenty years.

After I had met the fourth or fifth Mrs. Godbless, it struck me that many physics and chemistry departments had these women hanging around the edges of the department, haunting the premises like maiden aunts hidden away in back bedrooms who come shyly into the kitchen or the living room for a family meal or when there are guests, not certain of their welcome, knowing they do not pay their way. This circumstance seemed most typical in departments where there was not a single woman either tenured or in a tenure track position.

Margaret Darnell is a sixty-three-year-old physiologist who received her Ph.D. in chemistry in 1935, and taught her subject for the next six years at a small college in her hometown. "The school was new, I worked as an associate, I was a bright little thing, they treated me like a mascot. No trouble at all. Then I went out into the real world. My husband, he's a lawyer, decided to join a firm in the Midwest. When we got where we were going—which was the state university's hometown—I went to the school and asked for a job. The head of the chemistry department looked at me in amazement. He said to me, 'Mrs. Darnell, we don't hire *women* here. Go home and take care of your husband.'

"A few months later the Japanese attacked Pearl Harbor and the United States was at war. The chemistry head calls up and says, 'Mrs. Darnell, it's your patriotic duty to report to work.' 'Dr. Buller,' I say, 'I took your advice. I went home and took care of my husband. I'm pregnant.' 'Mrs. Darnell,' he says, 'we need you.' One day I was a flower of American womanhood, the next I was a peasant told to drop her baby in the fields and report for work. I taught chemistry throughout the war. Of course, I got the sack the day after the armistice was signed."

Annie Morris is a forty-seven-year-old physical chemist who recently lost a five-year battle for tenure. For Annie the struggle for tenure was a recapitulation of her lifelong sense of herself as an outsider in chemistry, one who barely holds on, knows her hold to be precarious, and knows further that one day she must slip and fall.

Annie is overweight and moon-faced. She wears round glasses, has a slightly fixed stare, a soft southern blur in her speech, a headful of flat, wiglike curls, and a manner altogether awkward and socially maladept. But when she starts talking science the awkwardness disappears, the face takes on definition, the body pulls itself together, the voice is altered by the unmistakable sound of intellectual authority.

I once heard two scientists discussing Annie's denial of tenure. One said, "Well, you've got to admit, she *is* odd, and it is understandable that people might not want to have an eccentric around for twenty years." The other one replied, "Come off it. There are guys in that department who are social basket cases. They wheel them in in the morning, close the lab door behind them, then take them home quick, they shouldn't scare the students. She's a brilliant chemist. If she's a crazy lady now, you'd better believe they *made* her one. She never knew what hit her from the first day she entered academic science."

She was raised in a family of coal miners. She played near the fields and wanted to know why there were rainbows in the coal. Her grandfather, who adored her, brought home a chemistry book. By the time she was in high school she had a chemistry lab, which she had built by herself in the cellar, and all the freedom she could handle in a high school where there were not too many like her. She went to a Midwestern state university, did very well in chemistry, and was admitted to CalTech. The only woman in the class, she blundered her way through social and intellectual ostracism ("You know, scientists are the most socially unskilled people in the world, and if you're a woman, and a chemist besides, you *really* don't know what's happening"), and accomplished two acts of some importance: She married Jim Morris, a fellow student, and she graduated first in her class.

The year was 1959. Jim Morris, who had graduated a third of the way down in the class, received fourteen job offers. Annie could not get a job. She was offered work as a technician, she was offered research associateships, she was offered fellowships on Jim's grant. At CalTech no one lifted a finger to help her.

Recalling that time, her voice takes on the slow-witted disbelief of a Jew in Czarist Russia wandering about, bleating, "But they *said* if I won the gold medal I'd be all right." And indeed, she does look half mad as she says, very softly: "You know? They lie. I mean, they just lie. They say if you do good you'll be rewarded. And they're *lying*. They're lying, and it never occurs to you that that can be the case."

I asked Annie if she had considered taking any of the fellowships or associateships? The crazy lady disappeared, and the grownup woman hardened. "Hell, no," she said curtly. "I was first in my class at CalTech."

At last an offer came from a chemical research foundation in the Midwest. Jim got a job in industry in the same city and off they went, relieved and happy. When she arrived at the foundation Annie discovered the job was really that of technician in the lab of a pharmacologist. Twenty years after the fact her voice becomes dazed. "I couldn't believe they were doing this to me. Not only was it a technician's job, it was technician to an *incompetent*. This guy wanted me to run experiments to prove something two equations on a piece of paper could disprove in the time it took to write them down. That was one of the lowest points in my life, when I realized why they had brought me out here.

"But I knew I had to stay. There was no place for me to go. So then I had to work my way, with guile and a political savvy I had to learn, into a real job at the foundation where supposedly a job was mine by right. I worked there in total isolation. The place was openly sexist, and I was a permanent oddity. The men ate in a dining room that permitted only men. I was not allowed in the dining room. Once a chemist from Scotland came especially to see me. The others at the foundation wanted to have lunch with him, too. They *still* wouldn't let me into the dining room. My colleagues had to run around and find an outside place to eat so I could join them. Most of these men were decent enough sorts. But nobody could even *imagine* challenging the system.

"It was the pits. Working like that. They had said to me,

'If you become pregnant you'll get fired.'" Annie's eyes get her crazy-lady glint in them, and she says softly, so softly: "Can you imagine what it means to hear something like that? I mean, that says something *deep* to you. About what you *are*.

"So I got pregnant, and they never knew it. I just wore a lab coat one size larger. Who ever really looked at me? I came back two days after the baby was born, and I never told a soul there that I had had a child."

It went on like this for years. At last she was offered a job at the state university in the city where they lived. She thought that was the end of her troubles in chemistry. She had grants, publications, citations, and her research had gained her an international reputation—but tenure was denied her. She took the university to court. Later, in the heaps of trial papers, there was a copy of a letter sent by her department chairman to three eminent chemists. The letter said, in effect: "We don't like her, and we don't want her; what would you do?" Each of the chemists had replied: "Give her tenure." But they did not. She could not find another job. Although she had a grant, she had nowhere to take it. Research chemistry was over for her.

In 1960 chemistry department heads said as openly as they had in 1940: "We don't hire women." In 1980, of course, no one would dare say this. Yet, at one of the great research universities one of the Mrs. Godblesses told me: "The chemistry department here doesn't advertise. It's illegal now, but they still do it that way. Somehow, they consider it a 'shame' to advertise. They write to their friends. And of course their friends are men who have only male graduate students. But even so, some awfully good young women get through the system and come up here for interviews. It's always the same. They look at these excellent young women and they say, 'She's very good but she lacks seasoning. Let her go off somewhere else for the year and then we'll consider her again.' Of the young men just like her they say, 'We'd better grab him before someone else does.' "

"My mother said, 'Be a scientist,' but she didn't really mean it"

Anne Polsky, thirty-eight-year-old molecular biologist, daughter of a lawyer and a music teacher: "My mother said, 'Be a scientist,' but she didn't really mean it. What she really meant was, 'Get married and teach high school biology so you can be a help and a pride to your husband.' When I took science seriously she felt betrayed."

Lillian Delgado, thirty-six-year-old chemist, daughter of working class immigrants: "My mother was an unhappy woman who lived through her three daughters. When we were young she said to us, 'In this world there are somebodies and there are nobodies. You've got to be a somebody.' Oddly enough, to her that meant becoming a doctor or a lawyer. But it was pure fantasy, something she'd picked up from forties movies; she didn't have the vaguest idea of what it was all about. She thought we should *get* the medical or law degree, but she didn't think we should really *use* it. She thought we'd be these classy mothers and wives who did a little law or medicine on the side. When I became serious about chemistry she was against it, and gave me a hard time. But it was too late. She'd already instilled drive and will in me. She didn't understand when she did it that she wouldn't be able to control it."

Alice Albright Williams, forty-three-year-old neuroanatomist, descended from a distinguished New England family: "My father was a scientist, my mother was his technician. I was sent to Radcliffe in the expectation that I would become a doctor. I was miserable in Cambridge and when I read Henry

Adams who told me it was men's deepest need to achieve and women's to nurture, I said, 'Aha!' and went looking for a husband. When I called home to say I was getting married my father was devastated. 'Darling,' he said. 'I thought you'd get your degree first and *then* marry.' You see, all the wives in our family are accomplished. Years later, when I got divorced and became a serious scientist, my father demurred, 'Darling, what about the children?' "

Every woman receives a mixed message about love and work in her youth. For most, the contradiction is paralyzing. The control required to work well becomes diluted and evaporates.

Self-disciplining of a highly individual nature was required of women drawn to the arts or the humanities, but the structure of science was powerful, and forced upon women who were potential scientists a rigor of working habits that ultimately (even against the childish and anarchic will) made them into productive and disciplined workers; among the scientists the mixed message most often backfired.

Still, the message was given and it was often sufficiently received to prove immensely retarding. Among the scientists, as well as among all other women, thousands experienced an unraveling of nerve over the question of work and love—or, more accurately, career and marriage. Some of the most forlorn women in science are now those in their forties who received Ph.D.s in the sixties, then got married and tried to build a working life around their marriages. They are the lost women scientists.

But this is indeed a "time of struggle," and many now are being admirably "timely."

Jessie Snyder is a forty-year-old botanist/ecologist whose office walls on the top floor of the natural history building of a Southwestern university are covered with huge photographs of a tropical cactus plant the size of a tree. This plant grows for two hundred years, blooms for one or two years, then dies. Jessie—her hair the color and texture of straw, her eyes ice blue, her body lanky and muscular, her face prematurely weathered—stares lovingly at the photographs. She jams her white cotton blouse back inside the belt of her blue jeans, picks up a pencil to gesture with and begins talking. "The questions we ask are: What evolutionary pressures gathered to create this in nature? What in the surround contributes to the life of this organism? What is the nature of the development of the reproductive system of such plants? These are questions that interest us. We are whole-organism biologists, looking at everything around the organism as well as everything in it.

"These, of course, are ultimate questions. There are other questions to ask in ecology, and some of them interest me, and I cultivate those interests because they're the ones that will get me funding. For instance, the questions asked in population plant biology." Jessie turns to another photograph on the wall, one that shows groups of trees growing together in thick clumps in small spaces in the forest. She explains that because of the low wind dispersal of seeds, most of these are baby trees that grew very close to the mother tree. It also appeared that most of these trees were dying and no one could figure out why. Jessie discovered that a massive fungal infection emanating from the mother tree was killing off the ones growing close beside her; the ones whose seeds the winds had thrown farther away were surviving. This is the kind of information valued and supported in Jessie's field, and so she does some of this sort of work. "But these questions are not the ones that interest the most, it's the evolutionary questions that grab you."

A tropical plant specialist who spends half the year in the

tropical rain forests of South America, Jessie Snyder is so entirely the hardworking scientist whose interior life is wrapped around "these questions" that it comes as something of a jolt when she casually announces: "It's only in the last two years that I am able to say to myself, I'm a scientist. Whatever it is that scientists do, that's what I do. It's only just now that I have the courage to be what I am."

She was born and raised in a small town in Minnesota and sent to a second-rate college in the middle of the state where that famous twin message—you can't be smart and still be a woman—went out strongly and was strongly received. She decided to become a high school science teacher because she had always been good at observing nature, went off to a nearby state university to receive a Master of Arts and Education in Science ("A silly degree that doesn't make you either a teacher or a scientist"), and went out into the world to teach. She hated it—hated the kids, hated the high school, hated teaching. Inside herself, aimlessness amounted nearly to desolation.

She met a man she liked who was living in Washington. She went West ostensibly to try teaching there but really to be with him. Through this man she came to live with a group of *National Geographic* types on a farm outside of Seattle, and it was here, at this time—she was thirty—that her fine sense of natural history suddenly took a swift and developing leap forward. With these people she began to watch plants and animals like a nineteenth-century "describer"; or like an agriculturist; or like a veterinarian; or like a plant biologist collecting specimens—all of whom coexist in her. The relationship with the man dissolved, but Jessie was newly put together. She entered the University of Washington as a Ph.D. candidate in ecology; within the year her life fell into place:

"All those false starts I made. I didn't know how to become a serious worker. Somewhere in my psyche I was hovering all those years, in limbo, expecting to become a wife and mother who also worked, but not too seriously, one who might perhaps go back to work after the children were grown as my mother had done. I just couldn't get it together, I'm sure, because I think (although I wasn't conscious of it) I was waiting for the right man to come along and make my future cohere."

She has had a number of love attachments over the years, and marriage proposals as well, but she has always felt, she says, with every man she's known that she couldn't really be herself: She was never completely there, some vital part was always missing. "Thank heaven, that always stopped me from marrying." She has a lover now, an ecologist at another university who shares her work. Deep into the green heart of Peru and Panama, Jessie and her ecologist-lover go to collect and to classify the largest rain forests in the world. Only here does he know who she is and, more important, does she know who she is.

Marilyn Ames is a forty-one-year-old endocrinologist who runs a lab in a cancer research center in Boston. One of her great skills as a scientist lies in knowing everyone in her field (who is doing what and where), reading everything that is written, and remembering everything she reads. She knows, for instance, that there is a scientist in Los Angeles who has a particularly excellent strain of cell culture that she needs, and that there is a man at Bell Labs whose technique for purifying the cell culture is extremely reliable. She will remember this when they are doing a particular series of experiments in her lab, and will get on the phone and arrange for these two elements to be brought to her aid.

At the same time that the cell culture in Los Angeles and the technique at Bell Labs is on her mind, it is also on her mind that she must make herself available to her four-to-seven workers, raise grant money, oversee experiments, replace lost or broken equipment, know what is going on in her lab eighteen hours a day. And she does so gladly, eagerly, with the pleasure of one for whom the all-encompassing business of doing science is only recently arrived at.

Marilyn Ames is a classic scientist delayed by the mixed message a woman receives in early life. She was raised in a suburb of Hartford. Both her parents were doctors, but her mother was devoted to her husband ("She practiced medicine on the side"). From the time she was a little child Marilyn knew she wanted to be a scientist; her absorption with observing nature systematically, and through experimentation, was fully developed by the time she was ten. At home her parents enjoyed their pretty little girl "being scientific" as though she possessed a clever trait that might make her a more interesting wife, just as mother's being a doctor had made *her* a more interesting wife. In high school Marilyn won the national science medal. Her father answered the phone when the news came and kept saying into it, "What is this, some sort of joke?" while Marilyn, almost in tears, pulled at his sleeve and kept shaking her head no, it wasn't a joke.

She wanted to go to Radcliffe where she knew she would get a good education. Her parents said no, they wanted her to be a lady. They insisted on Smith. "I guess from that moment on I was lost. When I didn't oppose them on the Radcliffe issue the die was cast." She married directly upon graduation and went out to California with her husband. "Luckily" he agreed that Marilyn might enter graduate school. She worked hard, but always around her marriage, and eventually got her degree. They came back east to New Haven because of her husband's work. "Luckily" she landed a good job at a medical research institute. Her marriage fell apart and she remarried, this time a Boston businessman. She moved to Boston and "luckily" went to work at the cancer research center. Her point with all these "luckily"s is that at any given moment she was prepared to move, or to stop working, or to accept the inability to advance in her work, if it meant imperiling relations with her husband.

Some years into her second marriage she and her husband went to Europe together. At a scientific conference in Paris Marilyn heard an American scientist speak, and she fell in love with his mind. She turned to look at her businessman husband and thought, Why am I married to him? She left her husband, took a leave of absence from the research center, and went out West to live with the scientist she had heard speak in Paris: "Even though I knew it was detrimental to my work, and certainly to my career, I felt I had to do this. I had to see if I could make a life with this man. That seemed infinitely more important to me than my work."

Within a year—she was now in her late thirties—she was wandering about in a daze, repeating to herself, What am I doing? What *am* I doing? "I had suddenly realized that the scientist was an arrogant bastard, a self-involved man who enjoyed the status of having a scientist for a mistress, but certainly did not take her work and her career as seriously as he took his own. When I was invited to give my first paper in Europe, and I was delirious with joy, he said to me, 'Ah, what do you want to go for? It's all show, anyway.' I said to him, 'For you it's nothing. You've been through it a hundred times. For me it's a lot, it's prestige and recognition and fun.' He said he wasn't going, and he didn't want me to go either. I went, but he wouldn't come. Not even to keep me company when I wanted him to."

She left him then and came back to Boston to the research center where she has been a hard-driving scientist ever since. She is now a woman of affairs—"I cannot and will not live without a man"—but they are conducted around her work, or they are not conducted at all. "It's not an ideal life"—she shrugs—"but it's a helluva lot better this way than the other way."

Julia Waxman is a thirty-eight-year-old biophysicist, originally trained as a high-energy physicist, who this past year was tenured in the physics department of a Northeastern university where she had worked for years as a research associate. It is almost a certainty that Julia was tenured because the university feared she was about to leave and take her highly prized physicist husband with her. Julia is very tired, and doesn't really *give* a damn anymore why the university gave her tenure.

She was born into a family of enlightened orthodox Jews. The atmosphere at home was gentle, loving, intelligent, timid. Both parents adored education and expected the girls as well as the boys to become professional workers. The children were all stamped to one degree or another with this expectation.

In her second year in college Julia discovered the beauty of physics, felt compelled by it, and decided on physics as her life's work. She was admitted to graduate study at Brown where she was the only girl in the class. Which did not bother her at all; like so many others, Julia says she never noticed it; she is the kind of guarded, inexpressive woman who makes a perfect candidate for the "I never noticed" school.

At Brown she met and married Barry Waxman, her male counterpart: smart, gentle, religious. Barry had just completed his dissertation when they met. Halfway through her degree, he received a post-doctoral fellowship at Harvard. Julia was admitted to Harvard as a grad student and followed him to Cambridge. After one year at Harvard Barry received his job at this university. Julia, of course, came along with him. Here she had their first child and slowly finished her degree at Harvard through the mail.

There was, of course, no job for her. She went to work at

the university as research associate to a biophysicist. In time she left high-energy physics and became a biophysicist herself. The years passed. She had another child. By all accounts her work was superior but no job could or would be found for her. Barry felt for her, but neither one of them was in the habit of making demands. They simply didn't see anything for it but to accept as a given the position in which they found themselves.

More years passed. Then, she says mildly, she fell into depression. "What form did your depression take?" I ask. Very quietly she says: "I began not to want to go out. I didn't want to meet people who were visiting the university. I was always explaining why I was where I was, always in these peripheral positions. I began to feel bad about myself. I didn't want to have to explain myself anymore. If I was good, people's eyes seemed to be saying to me, why didn't I have a job? And I agreed with them. It began to eat at me.

"Finally, Barry and I agreed that I would look for a job, and that he would get one where I got one. As soon as I went looking I found a job. NIH made me a fantastic offer, one that made everyone here sit up and take notice. I came to the department and I told them if they didn't give me a job I'd be leaving. They didn't say yes and they didn't say no. After all these years here. They waited until the last possible minute. I had three days to tell NIH whether or not I'd come. And then the department said okay, they'd give me tenure.

"Sometimes I'm a bit sorry they capitulated. It would have been easier to start all over some place fresh. Here, I suddenly became the head of a research group of which I had simply been a part. The grad students—who looked on me as one of them!—resented it. And then there's been the difficulty of learning how to carry a full teaching load—as well as learning how to organize and run a lab. I didn't know how to do any of it. It's best to learn those things when you're younger. I have difficulty, great difficulty with it. I'm exhausted all the time."

Julia Waxman smooths her good wool skirt of an unfashionable length across her knees. Beneath her thick unshaped hair, neat, unadorned features announce: Take no notice of me. Pretend I'm not here. I want no trouble. I'd rather die than seem aggressive or unladylike, say or do anything anyone might interpret as rude or offensive. Yet, at the end of our time together, when I ask this timid, unadventurous woman, "If you had it to do all over again would you do it the same?" she shakes her head without hesitation. "Absolutely not. If I had it to do all over again I'd certainly not do what I did. I wouldn't follow Barry. I'd have had a job of my own from the start. It's been very bad for me. Bad for me as a person. Bad for me as a scientist."

Janet Moran, twenty-eight years old, a botanist/ecologist in training, is Jessie Snyder's graduate student. Tall, skinny, goofy; blue-jeaned, frizzy-haired, wearing tinted granny eyeglasses. A child of her generation, Janet has moved from small-town Republicanism to membership in a farming commune to activism in a university town collective to leadership of encounter groups to graduate studies in science. She's all smart-ass cool; her two favorite words are "neat" and "nerd"; they apparently account for all things good and all things bad.

Born and raised in Iowa, Janet was the smartest kid in town. She loved goofing off, being sassy and popular, and always able to talk her way out of trouble. She also loved plants and the outdoors, loved watching the way things grew, was more systematic in her observations than she consciously knew.

Went to Iowa State; science courses were for fun; was going to take engineering and "make bucks"; left engineering three days after she started; got disoriented; dropped out; started living with a boy from high school; left him; went back to school, this time to the university at Ames; was drawn repeatedly to botany and ecology courses for the healing fun of it; took chemistry and physics because you couldn't learn more biology, ecology, and plant life without them; never saw herself as a scientist, was just fooling around "in science"; dropped out again; went West to join friends living in a collective in Oregon, learned fast about "groups"; was fascinated by power (still is), how it worked among people; drifted back to Ames after a year; lived in a group house; started baking bread in a collective; was soon managing the collective; after a while went back to school (it just seemed more interesting); graduated finally with a double major in botany and biology; drifted again; again lived in a group house, got involved in running encounter groups, suddenly saw it was "either groups or science." For the first time she said to herself, I'm not fooling around in science. I am a scientist. She came to the Southwest to become Jessie Snyder's student.

Still addicted to group houses, Janet leans back in a painted kitchen chair on a Saturday morning, while five other grad students are in varying stages of making breakfast, and has no trouble reflecting on her recent years:

"For a long time I thought I didn't want to be a scientist because I couldn't stand other scientists. They all seemed like such nerds. They were so humorless, so narrow, most of them had such tiny sights set for themselves. They seemed to say no to so much in order to say yes to so little. They don't know anything about anything. They don't know life is sex and power. They don't know biology is sex and power. They're scared of sex so they don't know.

"I still think all this is true. But I realize now that's not why I didn't want to be a scientist. I didn't want to become a scientist because I was scared myself. I could never imagine myself a college professor. Who, me? Become an adult? Nah. What're ya kidding? Not me. I'm too nearsighted. Or too short. Or too something. Maybe too much of a girl. Yeah. Maybe that's it. Somebody's gonna come along someday and take care of me. I don't really *have* to do this stuff. I'm just killing time, having fun, goofing off."

Her chair comes crashing down on the kitchen floor. "But god, I think I see it coming." She pushes her granny glasses back into place, flashes a huge grin, and says brashly: "This past year I realized I'm gonna be a star. I went on a field trip with other ecologists, and I saw. I'm brighter than most of them, and my scope is wider. Much wider. I'm interested in ultimate questions, not approximate ones. Not why does a plant grow in this much daylight, today in this place, under these conditions, but rather, what happens to the whole system if you kill this plant or grow that organism? What are the historic reasons, the evolutionary pressures that make this or stop that? Why has it been growing like this, and not like that? What's the history, the ecological history, of this condition or that?" She grins again. "Science became so much more fun once I stopped thinking someone was gonna come along and take care of me."

Recognition at Last: The National Academy of Sciences

Vivian Davidson is a fifty-nine-year-old geneticist who as a graduate student in the 1940s had already earned an international reputation for the research she was then doing, and would continue to do for the next twenty years and more. Two years ago she was elected to the National Academy of Sciences. The Academy has a membership of thirteen hundred. Of that thirteen hundred perhaps twenty-nine or thirty are

women. Of that twenty-nine or thirty almost all were elected
within the past six or seven years.

The scroll that Vivian received from the Academy had her
name engraved on it, and then went on to announce that Vivian Davidson was being honored for "his" accomplishments,
and that "he" was now entitled, and "he" could, and "he"
should. She was so amazed by all the "he"s that she sent a letter to the Academy inquiring whether the source of the problem might be that the engraver was British and had taken
Vivian for a man's name, or was it perhaps that the printing
process was lagging behind the process of election of women
to the Academy. The letter she received back from the Academy secretary (a man) was an angry one informing her that
she was the first person ever to complain, the scroll was an
honor, its plate had been struck in 1868 by Abraham Lincoln,
and it had a historic value the Academy was not about to tam-
per with.

At the next Academy meeting in Washington, Vivian raised
the matter of the scroll's wording with some of the other women
scientists. Each one said she had never noticed the use of "he"
instead of "she" on the scroll. "That's probably true," Vivian
said sadly. "They're so grateful to be allowed into the club,
they wouldn't dream of making waves. In all likelihood they
haven't noticed."

I told the story of Vivian Davidson and the Academy scroll
to a group of scientists at a party in Woods Hole in the summer of 1980. One woman in the group was a member of the
Academy. When I reached the end of the story, and everyone
was either gaping or laughing, this woman—thin, whitehaired,
chain-smoking—said coldly: "That is absolutely untrue. I have
a scroll and I'm quite sure it doesn't say 'he.' " The party fell
silent. The woman stared at me, I stared at her. There was
nothing for me to say. The following October I received a

postcard from her. In a scrupulously neat small hand she had written: "I want to apologize to you. I looked at my scroll when I got home. You were right. It *does* say 'he.' "

As of this writing the scroll still reads "he," there are still only thirty-odd women in the Academy, and most of them are still grateful to have been allowed into the club.

PART THREE

Women in Science:
Demystifying the Profession

Group Portrait: 1980

Imagine a group portrait of scientists of a hundred years ago. The picture is an oil painting made, after many formal sittings, by the Academy painter. The scientists are all dressed in black frock coats and striped pants, and they all hold themselves tall and stiff. But looking closely, one sees a dreaminess around the eyes of this one, a willfulness in the mouth of that one, a pair of flared nostrils over here in the corner, depression over there in the back row. It is a genuine group: individuals lifting themselves out of types.

Imagine this same portrait being made today of a group of scientists who are women. The picture, of course, is not an oil painting, it is a photograph. The harried photographer has had to snatch a moment from the hardworking day of white-coated women hurrying about a lab building, and he certainly will not have been able to get "everyone" because everyone will not have been around on the day he came to photograph. It is all very difficult, not at all leisurely or respectful, but at last the picture is taken and the print made. The surprised viewer observes a remarkable resemblance to the painted men of a hundred years ago: The white coats and the informal posture are leveling, but the faces give back individual differences. The viewer stares at the photograph for a long moment, aware that this is a historic document.

*   *   *

In the past, differences in style, personality, character were not permitted women scientists, and so none were exhibited. A woman scientist of only thirty years ago was a lady eccentric, a denatured bluestocking, a nineteenth-century New Woman. She wore tweeds and oxfords, cared nothing for love, kept a cat, and smoked cigarettes. Adopting the style of the gentlemen scientists among whom they worked, these women acceded in a socially repressive atmosphere to an even deeper repression of the self.

An overwhelming majority of the women scientists I spoke with who were between the ages of sixty-five and eighty-five conformed to the stereotype. Regardless of background or actual experience, there was about them a uniform remoteness of manner and expression. The pose was haughty and aristocratic, the speech guarded, the personality masked, defensive, unknowing. Each of them, in effect, said to me: "Problem? My dear, I *had* no problem. I knew what I wanted to do, and I simply did it." Caricatures of intellectual reserve and neutered sexuality, they would not discuss why they had never married, why they had worked as associates for fifty years, why they had been treated like den mothers and mascots by their colleagues.

Against this background it is startling and exciting to see, and to feel the presence of, a group of contemporary women scientists between the ages of twenty-five and fifty-five. It is the range of temperamental difference among them that sets the young women off from the old, reveals the meaningful passage of the generations. Even in outline, a group portrait of contemporary women scientists is ripe with a significant variousness. One sees women who are scientists occupying every position on a wide spectrum of personality types. Instead of concealing variety they seem to assert it. In fact, these women seem to reveal their individual selves through science rather than disappear into science as the earlier generation of women so often did. Come closer to the picture for a moment. Look directly into the faces of only a few of them. Observe them in some detail. The differences between them are quickly apparent. When you step back to view the group as a whole again, it is clear that something has changed, both in these women as women and as a representative group of contemporary scientists.

The organizing intelligence is instantly apparent, clearly there since childhood and brought to fruition in a life filled with compulsive sociability. She could be a functionary in a political revolution, a head nurse in a natural disaster, a leader of travelers lost in a jungle, or of survivors of a shipwreck. It's more than likely she became a scientist to organize a labful of people and equipment.

Lindasue Hearne is a thirty-year-old biopsychologist in the second year of a post-doctoral fellowship at a research institute in Washington. Small, sturdy, with Alice-in-Wonderland hair down to her waist and large blue eyes she bats mockingly, she was born and raised in a Southern town where, as she says, "the Spanish moss hangs out into the streets and the houses have white columns holding up the porch."

In her sophomore year at the state university she saw posted on a university bulletin board: "Do you like rats? If so, come up and see Dr. Ram." She went up, not because she liked rats, but because she was curious and liked the name Ram.

An Indian in a white coat said, "Yes?" Lindasue said, "I like rats. What's going on here?" Dr. Ram said: "We make electrolytic lesions in the ventromedial nuclei of the hypothalamus for the purpose of observing the effects of ablation on that part of the brain in the animal's feeling behavior."

At that moment another student walked in, said he liked rats, what was going on here? Dr. Ram turned to Lindasue. "Tell him," he said. Lindasue—who hadn't understood a word of what he had said—rattled back the sentences Dr. Ram had spoken. "You've got the job." Dr. Ram grinned.

After that Dr. Ram sat down with all the workers in his lab (graduate students, post-docs, technicians) and told them: "Everything you do in this lab is important. It's important that the rats be kept very well in order that they be useful in the experiments. It's important that the experiments go well in order to prove Dr. Ram's thesis. It's important that Dr. Ram's thesis prove out because Dr. Ram's life is on the line."

Two weeks later Lindasue walked into his office and said, "Dr. Ram, if your life is on the line let me tell you, you're in trouble. That lab is a wreck. Everything's filthy, nobody knows where anything is, the rats aren't fed regularly, nothing's labeled." One week after that she was running the lab; by the time she graduated she had written three papers with Dr. Ram. From then on she has been producing intelligent research and running knockout labs.

Shrewd, bossy, pragmatic, Lindasue Hearne is a scientist whose research serves the impulse toward "community" in its truest sense. She had loved Dr. Ram's little speech to his lab workers. It had made her feel part of a group with a mission, a member of a shared effort in a large ideal. She has never lost that feeling. Organizing the mission is her deepest drive. Not that Lindasue could transfer her organizing drive to political campaigns or community centers. No, it is only science that ignites her and induces in her the conviction of significance necessary to activate the missionary zeal that characterizes her.

Donna Beene, a thirty-seven-year-old virologist, sits on a couch in the motel-like living room of a suburban tract house near a university town in the Northeast. The house has the air of never having had all the boxes unpacked. Just as well. Donna has been denied tenure, and although her husband Richard has received tenure, they'll be leaving this room any day now for another one just like it halfway across the country. The circumstance is a familiar one for the Beenes whose life is more strongly characterized by the uprootedness of the American professional class than it is by science, although science is what they each do wherever they go and, ostensibly, they go in order to keep on doing science.

Donna and Richard Beene have been married since their senior year in college. They were both born and raised in Los Angeles, the children of big business executives. Each of them has a strong sense of corporate flux. Their solidity resides in their own alliance, their loyalty to each other, to their children, to themselves as family-making adults. Within that context there has been a remarkable amount of evenhandedness between them about where they go for whose job.

Donna came to this university as a visiting professor. The title is a euphemism. It means a place is made in the department's laboratories for a scientific worker, but the worker must support him or herself wholly through grant money that he or she brings in. The university does not pay the scientist's salary, nor is there a promise or agreement that a tenured job will ever be offered.

Donna says that virology is altogether out of fashion right now in professional science; this year her grant proposal was refused support; her department, in turn, made it abundantly clear that she would not be offered tenure. She has a bitter and awed sense of the excludingness of the grant system, and insists angrily that the rewards inside the system of academic science are reserved for those who do what is fashionable (that is, that which will produce publishable papers and generate grant money), and are cruelly withheld from those who do not.

She has already been offered a job in industry, in a Midwestern city. If they can find a suitable job for Richard in the same city, it is pretty certain this is the job she'll take, even though it entails having to learn a whole new way of doing science. Pain, resentment, relief, and enthusiasm struggle together in her face as she describes what may lie ahead of her. "Doing science is just solving problems," she says. "Getting the answers. Learning new information. It's *all* science. All the problems are fascinating. Why shouldn't I do industrial science instead of virology? Especially if they'll reward me for it instead of punishing me."

Intellectual abstraction in science is not a source of happiness for Donna Beene. The idea of industrial science does, in fact, seem to suit her admirably. Somehow, it is not hard to imagine Donna in a white coat, holding up a smoking beaker, smiling into a camera while a voice in the background announces that here at Jackson Labs progress is our most important product. Like her engineer husband, Donna loves rolling up her sleeves and pitching into what feels like a "real" problem. Finding an immediate and applicable solution puts her at her cheerful best.

A huge Victorian pile stands on a spit of land jutting out into a bay on the Massachusetts coastline. All oxidized turrets, leaded windows, and brown-red brick, this building could easily have begun life as a nineteenth-century prison or asylum. It is now a research institute. The interior matches rather than belies the exterior. The corridors are long and dark, the laboratories small and crowded, and the equipment in them all much older than it should be. The men who walk the halls in white coats all seem bald, silent, socially speechless.

In a basement laboratory in this building a small, slim woman rules over a world of cages containing white rats with implanted bits of metal protruding from their soft confused skulls. All day long this woman inserts tiny needles in the rats, places tissue slices under the microscope, writes observations in a notebook. She works alone. From time to time a technician or a post-doctoral fellow comes to work with her but the arrangement is never successful; inevitably, she is alone again in the basement laboratory inside the brick building at land's end.

Gloria Honig is a forty-eight-year-old biochemist. Her parents were thorough, precise, inflexible. Whatever was socially fixed and acceptable was what the Honigs did, and whatever they did they did with excruciating thoroughness. Doing things with thoroughness usually meant doing them alone. No one could be depended on to perform a task as well as you could depend on yourself, and performing the task well was unquestionably the point of one's existence.

Some years ago Gloria became intrigued by the newly exciting field of opiate receptors in general, and then by morphine in particular. She taught herself pharmacology to learn how morphine affects the brain, and then devised an extremely exact method for injecting morphine into precisely the right place in a rat's brain in order to follow the path traced by the drug along the brain's neurons. This exactness involved the use of tiny needles, which she, and she alone, has perfected. She has never been able to teach anyone else to use the needles as perfectly as she uses them. So she works alone. She knows her situation is a rarity in modern science. "I've been told I work like a nineteenth-century scientist." She laughs nervously, as though she knows she is exposing herself to unsympathetic scrutiny.

Gloria is alone everywhere, not only in her lab, but at home and in the institute as well. She is married to a physicist whom she describes as kind, decent, intelligent, and reliable. "But," she says confidingly (slightly unhinged by so many questions being asked about herself), "I can't *speak* to him. Sometimes

I try to tell him what I'm feeling. He just stares at me. Then he goes into his room, closes the door, and spends the evening doing theorems."

Three years ago Gloria reported the head of the laboratory for keeping a relative of his, a part-time clerk, on the payroll as a research associate. Now she is a pariah at the institute, shunned by all those bald and silent men. Remembering this incident she remarks with sudden bitterness, "I was alone in this, all alone. Even my husband did not support me. But I couldn't stand to see such corruption go unchecked." Unchecked corruption is the equivalent of imperfect work: to be avoided at all costs. At all costs inevitably insures isolation.

She knows her talent, her skill, her scientific contribution will rest finally, and only, on the absolute cleanness and reliability of the slow, careful work she does all alone in this laboratory. From time to time—as when her husband closes his study door or her colleagues avoid her eyes in the hall—she imagines she is deprived of friends, lovers, associates. But in fact these people represent emotional distractions she must strip herself of if she is to be happy—poring in obsessive lonely intentness over the rats, the microscope, the notebooks—doing the task well the only way the task can be done well: with excruciating thoroughness.

Contrast Gloria Honig with Lindasue Hearne. In each case science feeds an extreme, idiosyncratic personality, allows it to nourish and fulfill itself. Interesting that "the extremes" are at opposite ends of the psychological spectrum.

The room is lovely, a whitewashed rectangle, high-ceilinged, studded with oak-framed windows; at one end a baby grand piano set off by a plank floor painted white; at the other end a small sitting room: Oriental rug. Victorian sofa covered in beige velvet, two upholstered hard-backed chairs. Against the wall halfway between the sofa and the piano, a black walnut chest supports a mass of spring flowers arranged beautifully in a fat ceramic jar. On the sofa sits a woman as lovely as the room she has composed: white-skinned, black-haired, a face out of a medieval Italian painting.

The woman on the sofa is a thirty-two-year-old cell biologist. We are speaking together on a Sunday afternoon. As the hours pass she begins to glance repeatedly at her watch; she has an experiment going in her lab, it must be checked like an infant every four hours, she'll have to leave soon.

Veronica Satino was born and raised in a middle-class suburb where everyone had been a blue- or white-collar worker the day before yesterday. Veronica was energetic, pretty, and smart. She enjoyed solving the problems in math, and the theorems in physics, partly because her facility was so obvious, but mainly because it made her special (not special-freakish but special-privileged), gave her an edge (none of the other girls was good at science), an extra excitement that increased her confidence, made her secretly arrogant. In the beginning that is what doing science meant to her—it gave her social cachet, fed her sexual vanity, enlarged the power to attract. But that was in the beginning.

"Throughout graduate school," Veronica muses, smoothing the beige velvet beneath her slim hand, "whenever I had to choose between breaking a date and going back to the lab to work late—either to collect data or observe an experiment in progress or get the results of an experiment series—I always felt guilty about the broken date, and as often as not didn't go back to the lab.

"It's a crucial moment in the making of a scientist, that moment when all other concerns capitulate to the need to go back to the lab, and in most women, I suspect, that moment is delayed. For me, it didn't come until long after I had graduated. But when it came, I not only broke a date, I forgot all about it, stayed in the lab until midnight, and only when I was walking home remembered the guy. That night I became a scientist."

After that night, Veronica says, she discovered science love; the love that culminates repeatedly in the special thrill that comes when an experiment yields up a significant finding. She, too, defines the moment as incomparable, and speaks of what it feels like to walk around with a scientific discovery inside you that you've told no one else about: "It's not that you're thinking of seeing your name on the front page of the *New York Times*. It's that you've got this secret. You know something about the universe no one else knows."

Note the arrangement and the syntax of Veronica's last sentences. From a woman at all times aware of the social-sexual-political equation: the first reference is to the *New York Times,* the second to the secret of the universe. Naked admission of the mixture of worldly ambition and intellectual passion struggling up (always in a different configuration) in every scientist.

Marina Markman is a fifty-three-year-old physicist. Tall, thin, Nordic-blond, with a gawky stringiness in the neck and upper body, hers is the grave beauty of the ugly duckling. The high intelligence that breaks repeatedly through the straining squint, the unexpected openness of speech, the profound courteousness of manner combine to create an essence of civilized discourse that, hour by hour, deepens the pleasure one takes in her company, and makes of her a radiant presence.

Marina is the daughter of a famous scientist, and theirs was a classic attachment—the educated father whose closest companion was this intellectual daughter. Marina adores her father even now. "My father was a great man," she says, "and he took me along. He said everyone should do something that was interesting to them, and at which they could make a living, and that this was as true for women as it was for men. I think my father's saying that stayed with me through everything. Although," she adds, suddenly staring off into the floor, "when it came to it, my father's idea of success for me was teaching physics in a small women's college out of the mainstream. I think he thought that would be less hurtful to me. But it was the wrong thing to tell me."

As I listen to Marina speaking in her low, measured, unintrusive voice, I think from time to time of how our mutual friend (another teacher at Marina's university) has told me that at faculty meetings Marina sits knitting like Madame Defarge, brusque and impatient with the most ordinary infraction if it comes from a man. "There's a chemist," our friend said, "an old man. It takes him forever to make his point. And he also begins making it in the middle of some-one else's sentence. It's annoying. But he's an old man. Marina can't stand it for one second. She immediately says: 'Mr. Chairman, I thought we were operating by established rules here. No interruptions, and you've got ten minutes to speak. Would you kindly inform Professor Wheeler of the rules so the rest of us need not be imposed upon?' God! The years of stifled anger behind that courteous exterior."

She learned Latin and Greek, was good at French, the classics, anthropology. One of these was her intention. Determined never to compete with her father, she didn't even know if she liked science (the subject was psychologically forbidden), but in her second year at Smith she looked through a microscope and decided instantly on chemistry.

"Why?" I ask, startled at the firmness of the remark.

Marina's long neck grows longer; her head inclines to one side; she pushes her glasses up onto the narrow bridge of her thin nose; her eyes squint. "Because it was real to me," she says quietly. "I looked through the microscope, and the world became real, I knew I was looking at the real thing."

At Smith in 1948 everyone was preparing to get married, but if you were serious there were people to encourage you. Marina was serious. More to the point, she adds dryly, she was her father's daughter. She hasn't a doubt in the world as to why she was accepted as a Ph.D. candidate at a major university in the West. "As long as I wasn't hopeless they all had to do something for Daddy's daughter."

In 1952, having married another graduate student in physics, she received her degree. Her adviser said to her, "Well, now, we've got to get you a job, don't we? It seems to me a good job for you would be as editor of a scientific journal." Marina said, "I want to do research." The adviser stared at her. Plainly, his good offices as Daddy's friend had come to an end.

Marina and her husband came east to a university where he received a professorship and she a research associateship. They were at three different schools over the next years. It was always the same arrangement—he the professor, she the research associate. In 1965 her marriage fell apart and she went after the job she now holds—tenured professor at a celebrated research university. "Without the women's movement there is no doubt I would not have received tenure," Marina says in the same measured voice with which she spoke of having received decent treatment because she was her father's daughter.

She knows her life looks as though she has walked a royal road to easy success. She does not speak of the grinding loneliness her position has often imposed on her, the humiliations inflicted by the burden of privilege peculiar to women scientists related to Great Men in Science.

Why has she stayed with it?

The long, thin, graceful-awkward face, sometimes haggard in repose, is transformed by a grin—all inappropriate childish delight—breaking through the strain. "I couldn't give up the

real thing," she says. As she speaks the words "the real thing,"
I see how the ugly duckling became a swan.

Sitting behind a cluttered desk in a laboratory office high
up in a glass and steel building in the middle of an industrial
section of Philadelphia, a woman laughs often, gesticulates
freely, twists about in her chair. Her voice is eager, forthright,
articulate. Words pour, bubble, stream, shoot from her. Energy is clearly the commanding principle; that energy must be
given its head. One can easily see her turning hard, dominant,
overriding, madly pursuing the main chance; even easier to
see her as a girl on the streets of Philadelphia, a skinny bundle
of energy, arms and legs flying, hair swinging in every direction, all fierce vulgar hungriness, fighting off everybody in
sight to get hers; and she has got hers.

Carol Steiner is forty years old. Head of the genetics department at her prestigious medical school, where she was
once a student in this very department. When she graduated,
her boss suggested it would be a nice thing for her to now go
teach in a women's college.

"Oh, I don't want to teach in a women's college," Carol
replied. "I don't want that at all."

"What *do* you want?" the boss asked.

" I want your job," Carol shot back.

She leans forward across her desk, jabbing a forefinger
through the air at her visitor's vital center. "And I've *got* it."
Her laughing voice is edged with self-mockery, but only edged.

Carol's parents were a small-businessman and a school-
teacher. The father turned away from her when he realized she
was smarter than he was, but the mother lived through the
girl: proud, eager, interested in everything she might do or
become. Carol grins. "You only need one."

She had a kind of expectant nerviness that made her take on
everything in college—art, literature, philosophy. In her junior

year she attended a lecture in biology, saw an anatomy dissection, got excited, wanted to try it herself. She was told she could not do it. That was all she had to hear. She found a way into the class, learned how to do the dissection with a book on her lap and a specimen on the table in front of her, was accepted into an honors science program, took six science courses in a year, graduated with a double major in literature and science. But she knew she was a scientist: "When I look at that stuff from college now! My literature papers read like scientific analysis, and my science papers read like literature."

She came to work as a graduate student in this laboratory, and experienced immediate infatuation with the atmosphere of science—the lab, the equipment, the conversation, the compulsiveness. This was then one of the "hottest" genetics labs in the country. Smart, fierce, and hardworking, she was spotted immediately, and taken on.

The geneticist who then ran this lab is described by Carol as a loving, tender mentor whose manner is hard, cutting, challenging, insulting. This, she says, is deliberate: "If people can't take the heat they have to get out of the kitchen."

Why? I ask.

"Because if you can't take the psychic stress you can't compete."

Compete for what?

"The answers."

But if you keep working the answers will come.

"Ah, but the point is to get the answers *first*."

I stare at Carol a long silent moment.

"Look," she says, "that *is* the way it is. There's no point in pretending otherwise." She gathers herself into a burst of speech: "In every time there is a body of ideas around which important information is collecting. The best minds are drawn inevitably to these ideas, and are animated by the competition of contributing the *most* important piece of information, making the best synthesis, the finest analysis, *the* historic discovery. Now, in our time and especially in this place, that body of ideas is molecular biology. We stand at the edge of the new world, making a fire to light up the frontier, and we who are working in genetics are *in* the cauldron. We burn with it, go to sleep with it, eat, drink, taste, smell, and feel it all the time. And what keeps us going is, 'Maybe I'll get there first.' "

She does not think these attitudes unusual among scientists. She thinks she is an ordinary working scientist, and what is in her is common to many. She acknowledges that those with no taste for competitiveness often fall by the wayside in science, and *that* she thinks too bad, but on balance she thinks it fine that "we work hard, and we love science, and we want to get there first."

Merle Wyman, like Carol Steiner, feels the dynamic of research and competition as an interwoven excitement that runs through her like electric charge. In Merle, a thirty-four-year-old biochemist, the charge is openly eroticizing. A large solid woman with a mass of brown curls flying about her face, she walks down the halls of the New Jersey research institute where she works, dressed in jeans, boots, an open-necked shirt and no bra, moving with a suggestiveness that increases as she approaches her lab door. Merle gives the impression of striding across her earth in seven-league boots, all appetite and healthy aggression.

She worked as a graduate student in the laboratory of a scientist she describes as an empire builder: There were fifty projects going in the lab at all times. Merle wanted to do an experiment around an idea she had about a brain neuron. Her boss said sure, go ahead. Her experiment proved out, her thesis was validated. Her boss realized immediately that she had made an important discovery. Press conferences were called, grant proposals written, international meetings attended. The boss "took Merle along" on this trip, giving her work "almost" full credit. Then he was awarded an important prize for this piece of work, together with another pair of scientists who, like Merle and her boss, were a principal investigator and a graduate student also working on the same scientific problem. Merle alone was left out.

It is commonplace for the principal investigator to get the credit for a scientific discovery made in his or her lab, and for the graduate student whose work was vital to the discovery to be denied credit. This is part of the medieval tradition of master and apprentice that still prevails in science. But, like all else, the system is now breaking down.

Merle did what people in science do not do: She broke ranks and wrote a letter to the Prize Foundation, announcing that she had done the work. The letter was picked up by a reporter from a scientific journal, then by the newspapers, then by the women's movement. Overnight, Merle was famous. She had thought she might be committing professional suicide when she wrote to the Foundation, but as it turned out her strengths were consolidated and she prevailed. She came here to this institute where she has a huge lab, a fine grant, a job for her husband who is also a scientist, and the exercise of some real power. Merle loves the power, it makes her feel sexy as she walks down the hall. The source of this feeling is complex, not simple. She tries to explain. Leaning forward across her desk, over a sheaf of her scientific papers, she says:

"There are a million neurons in the brain, but nobody's ever known how *this* particular neuron works (she taps the pile of manuscript). I *do*. It's like nothing else in the world, in life, to know that. And what it took to *know* that. That's the process of discovery, that's the beauty of science. The idea, which precedes the design of the experiment, is everything. Yet, it is nothing unless someone has the strength and confidence to make it work, and to meticulously and laboriously accumulate the data necessary to convince other scientists to take the idea into their collective brain, and to work with it. That's *really* everything."

She stops a moment, moves restlessly about inside her clothes, tosses a pencil across her desk, crosses her booted legs, pushes her flyaway hair out of her eyes and bursts out: "But it's *all* of it together! There's no way to separate out the excitement, the discovery, the love of the brain, love of my own power, love of thought, love of science. It's all one and inextricable from the pressure, the competition, the gossip, the bitter fights over who discovered what first, the rush to print with an idea only half-substantiated, the grubby struggle over grant money, and then the extraordinary beauty of the biochemical printout, the awe of the tissue under the microscope, the graph that plots the crucial curve, the mapping of a neuron. It's enough to make you believe in God."

Everything about Merle Wyman is a vivid play on the classic man in science: the eroticism of power, the stabilizing mate, the association of scientific discovery with personal triumph, the public claim on recognition for an original piece of work. Very few women in science are put together in quite this way. Very few at this moment, that is.

The place exudes wealth and elegance—the furniture is velvet, the rugs Chinese, the lamps antique—and the woman pouring wine from "quite a good bottle of white"—beautiful, gracious, expensively dressed—seems the perfect model for the setting. Suddenly, a jarring piece of behavior and the atmosphere blurs. The woman sinks down on a velvet couch, throws her feet up on a marble coffee table, and groans. "What a day! I've done that experiment fifty times now, and *still* it won't come out. My boss is going to kill me."

Elizabeth Whitney is fifty-two years old. She received her Ph.D. in biochemistry a year ago, and is now halfway through a post-doctoral fellowship. Although this apartment is similar to apartments she has spent much of her adult life in—apartments from which she has taken both pleasure and a sense of identity—much of the time now her eyes glaze across these sumptuous rooms, her mind on the experiment in progress which she has left behind in the lab across town where she spends sixty to seventy hours a week.

Elizabeth was raised by her father, a small-town lawyer, after the mother whom she resembled eloped with another man; from the time she could remember her father talked to her as though she were a mental incompetent. She was also very beautiful, another piece of bad news; everyone wanted her, men and women alike, so she was either slavered over or scorned; either way, she remained isolated.

She did badly in school, floundering about, taking courses aimlessly. She sort of loved biology, though, had loved it even in high school, loved the way the various systems in the human body worked; they seemed beautiful to her. She found peace and pleasure in her biology courses—but she did not find context or purpose, direction or discipline.

She wandered out into the world, went to Chicago, got picked up by a sculptor at the Art Institute, and become a beautiful girl hanging around the Chicago art crowd. At twenty-two she was pregnant, married, and had settled into being an artist's wife for the next fourteen years. Feeling bored and useless at thirty-six, she decided to go to school just for the fun of it. She looked through envelopes of clippings she had idly collected over the years to see what interested her. To her surprise it was still biology. She enrolled at one of the city universities. From the first moment it was pure joy: "Biology was like having a whole lot of beautifully wrapped and beribboned boxes suddenly sprawling all over the bed, and you know, you just *know,* whichever box you open there's going to be a lovely surprise in it. No bad surprises. Only beautiful ones."

After the second semester the teacher said to her, "What are you doing here?"

"Just taking biology courses," Elizabeth said.

"Why?" the teacher asked.

"Because I love them," she said.

"You're too good for that," he said. "You should go on and take a Ph.D."

Those were the only words spoken to her, ever, by anyone, about her science career. With those words alone she put herself through four years of undergraduate school at night and then, well into her forties, through graduate school. Why? "No one had ever told me I was too good for anything. I couldn't let that go."

Her marriage dissolved. "You know what it was like in those years. Or perhaps you don't, perhaps you were lucky. My husband immensely resented my sudden love of school. He began accusing me of not caring for him and the children. His neck swelled like a bull, he grew red in the face, he loomed over me, this huge six-foot man, and he said loudly into my face, 'You *love* those courses, don't you? You can't fool me. You love them!' Then he said either I dropped out of school and we moved to the suburbs, or he'd leave. I thought, No matter what happens I can't do that."

Elizabeth looks around the room, smiling. "Now I live with this real nice man. He's a sweetie, and we're very fond of each other. But, I mean, God forbid, I should ever have to make choices. Let me put it this way. Once two things happened at once. A poet named Milton Klonsky wrote a book called *Shaking the Kaleidoscope.* It was all about the different shapes to an experience. At the same time that I was reading this book I heard Berta Scharrer, the German-born biologist, speaking on her work. There she was, this wonderful gracious woman of seventy talking with such simplicity and beauty of her work, presenting her theory and her findings. Afterward, someone, a young man, asked her rather sharply what she would do if her theory proved wrong. 'Oh,' she said, her face lighting up, 'wouldn't that be lovely!' I smiled at her and I thought, Shaking the kaleidoscope. The design will change but there will always be a design. That's what doing science means to me. Who could ever walk away from that?"

A beautiful woman in need of beauty, finding, through the scientist in herself, the mirrored promise of unending replenishment.

A summer's day on a sandy spit of land overlooking Cape Cod Bay. The roof of the house is New England mansard but the light and space within are summerhouse modern. The house buzzes with movement. Children, dogs, bicycles, showers, typewriters, refrigerators, and screen doors, all going at once. A woman emerges from a door on the side of the house: short, chunky, naked, five months pregnant. Her eyes are large, her hair tangled and sunstreaked, her mouth loose, her jaw slightly underslung. She stands on a wooden platform beneath an outdoor shower, turns the valves, throws back her head, and opens her mouth to receive full in the face the rushing stream that delights and revives.

Andrea Livewright is a thirty-seven-year-old geneticist at a large university four hundred miles south of the Cape. Her face and her body reflect the vitality of a free spirit coupled with an articulated appetite. She loves her husband, her children, her body; she loves music, politics, language; good food, sailing, swimming. Science is only a part of her life, never could it be the whole of things, it repels her to contemplate such a distortion of the act of living. For Andrea, that which makes you lose your appetite for life is to be turned away from.

Andrea received her degree from Harvard and then was asked to stay on, as very good graduate students often are: for the new blood and the cheap labor. The atmosphere at Harvard for the young assistant professor is both stimulating and demoralizing. Andrea remembers the latter more vividly than the former: "Harvard searches the world for the best, and it brings them back. So you've got a department full of famous people. Famous people do not necessarily like being one among the many. So they spend a lot of time demonstrating that they are more worthy of their fame than the next famous guy is of his. This produces an atmosphere of strain, cruelty, self-importance, and headache-giving demand. You are almost never able to enjoy or profit from that which made a man famous in the first place." Sitting on the beach on a gloriously clear day in August, Andrea rubs her forehead as though she is getting a headache just recalling what she is describing.

"I couldn't bear to do what everybody else does," she goes on. "Hang around waiting for the inevitable denial of tenure in the remote and wretched hope that it wouldn't happen to you. Meanwhile having your nerve and your self-respect drained, often beyond repair."

So she wrote a genetics textbook that was taken up for classroom adoption, got rich, went somewhere else and got tenure, divorced her husband, married another, continued with her research, and now runs around the world to biology conferences, enjoying life and engaging in debates in print on whether or not women in science can or should have families.

If all the parts were equal. But all the parts are not equal. They are not even interchangeable. Losing a husband is one thing, losing children another; losing certain kinds of pleasures, or responses, or interests, or circumstances is never the same as losing others. If life remained exactly as it is, and only science was lost it would be one thing, the other way around quite another. Life as a scientist only would be stark indeed, but life *without* science? Let's see now. How does that prospect sit with her?

Andrea bows her head for a moment, gazing out into the sand beneath her spread-eagled legs, then she looks up, stares out at the unbroken line of bay and sky, and shakes her head. "No," she says, "that would ruin the whole thing." She turns toward me, and her face breaks into a transforming smile. Delight overwhelms an expressive face. She explains why that would ruin the whole thing.

Andrea works on a single-celled organism which, as she puts it, stands at the fork between plant and animal life. "If I am asked *why* I work on this creature I say it is because it is an easy organism on which to try and discover how cells 'recognize' each other, and collect into the proper parts—the liver, the stomach, and so forth—and why it might be that cancer cells are cells that have 'failed' to recognize their 'place' and therefore collect in inappropriate places. That's what we tell them in the grant proposals, anyway. But the fact is"—she leans forward on the open beach as though she is about to give me secret information and it is necessary that we avoid hidden microphones—"I really *love* my organism," she says. "I love it because I've come to know it. Because I work *well* with it. Because it's as familiar to me"—she opens her hand in the air—"as the palm of my hand." She closes her hand into a fist. "It's mine," she says. "It's mine as nothing else is mine. And what happens when I'm possessing what is mine cannot happen anywhere else in life. Not for me, anyway.

"There is a satisfaction in suddenly understanding something about an organism you know well—why it does a particular thing, or acts in a particular way—that is indescribable and incomparable. No novel, or piece of music, or history of politics can reach me as this does. With this I feel I've been *active* in learning the truth. With all else I am a passive receiver."

Tall, slim, slightly horsey looking, with a smooth plain face whose separate beauties become apparent only slowly; as she moves about—speaks, listens, responds—one sees that the eyes are fine, the mouth sensual, the hair of a good weight. The plainness is self-assurance in careful repose: the work of a woman who has spent a great deal of time making sure she will not be caught off guard.

Maureen Shaw is a forty-three-year-old biophysicist, medical doctor, and administrator of scientific monies. She was raised in Kentucky, the daughter of a coal-mining engineer, and she always knew she would be an educated person. "Getting married wasn't something you *did*." Sent east to Barnard, her youthful interest in mathematics was encouraged and she ended her undergraduate course with a major in physics. After graduation she entered medical school: "At Barnard that just seemed the right thing to do. Did you know that one in twenty women doctors come from Barnard?"

In her last year in medical school Maureen married her husband, became pregnant on schedule (delivery planned not to interfere with last-year exams), moved up to Maine where her husband had obtained a university appointment and she an internship at the university teaching hospital. When the internship was completed Maureen realized she wanted to do research, not practice medicine. She obtained a joint appointment in biophysics and medicine in the medical school, and seven years later found herself embroiled in a bitter struggle for tenure. During this time she discovered that she was a political animal, and that she had a strong taste for running things.

The chairman of her department opposed her tenure. As it happened, this chairman was guilty of "misappropriation of funds" (getting money for one thing, spending it for another, something almost every administrator and bureaucrat is guilty of). Maureen wrote a report on the chairman, and he was brought up for investigation. According to Maureen, the chairman then became utterly disoriented.

"The thing was, he didn't know how to deal with me. I could see, he was at a total loss as to how to approach me. He couldn't figure out how I would react. I told a male colleague, whom the chairman didn't get along with either, 'With you he knows, or he thinks he knows, where your balls are. With me, it's a total unknown.'

"Basically, and this was the problem all the way through, he could not really conceive of a woman as anything but a hausfrau. No matter what he said, this came through repeatedly. If it had been a man he disliked, the whole thing would have gone forward very differently.

"He couldn't believe this was happening to him. So he'd call me up one night and, essentially, the conversation was, 'Maureen, you're doing such a wonderful job, you've got such beautiful blue eyes, will you go to bed with me?' The next night it'd be, 'Listen, I know things about you, don't think I don't, and I'm going to spill everything I know.'

"I was so surprised I became speechless. And then I discovered how effective my silence was. He'd say these things, and I wouldn't reply. There'd just be this long silence on my end of the line. And he began to fall apart. From there to tenure was one repulsively easy step."

Maureen ruminates with quiet satisfaction on the important lesson learned from this distasteful engagement of wills: "You've got to know when to cut it, and when to cool it, and women really *don't* know much about that sort of thing. In the matter of tenure, for instance, they really don't know that all the politicking has to take place in advance of the tenure decision. Once you've received a denial of tenure the ballgame's over. I learned a lot then, and I never forgot what I learned."

The politics of professional science has become Maureen Shaw's special province. The struggle for tenure, which taught her much about academic politics, prepared her for scientific administrative politics: who and where and how money, appointments, grants, and fellowships in the large scientific granting agencies will be disbursed. She has risen in this world, and has come to understand that the political shaping of the scientific profession is her true "field." This is where she thrives, where her strongest gifts of mind are applied, where science and real well-being feed into each other.

The women doing science today are characterized by their variousness. Among them are women with the personalities of data-collectors, and others with the personalities of philosophers. They are truth-seekers and problem-solvers, abstractionists and competitors. Temperamentally, they fill the range from the visionary and the isolate to the compulsively sociable and the rogue maverick. The psyche and character of most contemporary women scientists has been wonderfully shaped by their newfound ability to be scientifically accomplished while at the same time retaining the full flavor of their individual being. Science now provides each of them with a culture of the working self within which one is both free and defined. Exactly as men have always been.

At no moment before this have women scientists been free to be themselves; the exhibition of "temperament" and human variousness among them is a true event in scientific life; it signals a transformation; it means we have arrived at a point in the history of women in science where things may *look* as they have always looked (women half in, half out of science is still the greater truth), but enormous change is in process.

It is not to the advanced attitudes of professional science that we are indebted for this striking occurrence, but rather to the power and influence of contemporary feminism. If it is especially fitting that feminism—a social force whose limits have not been reached, and whose capacity for cultural consequence has not yet been fulfilled—should impress its urgency, its eloquence, its large meaning on science in particular. In the most significant of ways, they are meant for each other.

Feminism and Science

I was asked repeatedly: Do women do science differently than men? Do they work more intuitively? Do they act on their findings more readily or less readily? Do they think at a different pace, or employ a different sense of organization? Above all, do they ask different kinds of scientific questions, or develop different methods of inquiry?

This question is being asked now of all women entering the professions, and doing the kind of work previously done almost exclusively by men. It is a question that originates out of the old insistence that women are by nature unsuited to structured intellectual work, and mainly it is asked by those for whom the matter is one of pain and regret. The desired answer is, clearly, no.

There is, however, another group of people also asking this question who want the answer to be yes. Oddly enough, these people are feminist theorists. A special development in contemporary feminist thought posits the idea that the experience of women as such is special and palpable, that this specialness makes a unique contribution of the mind and spirit, that it has the capacity to carve out a different approach to intellectual life, and that its power is felt immediately women begin to take part in the common enterprise.

The experience of women-as-women is important and problematic. Once upon a time a woman delighted to be told that she thought or worked "like a man." Today, that always dubious compliment has become an epithet. It speaks alarmingly to a denial of the self. It disallows the impress of a woman's lived life on the style and the substance of work, as the impress of the lives of men-as-men has not been disallowed.

But what constitutes a lived life? If there is a characteristic "maleness" in various modes of thought and work it is the outcome of hundreds of years of assimilated experience. As a class of being—regardless of loss, failure, or defeat—men have walked the earth as though they owned it. There is bold aggression and a surfeit of self-confidence in the way in which many men work because most men have expected that an achieved life was theirs by right. Linked to this expectation, aggression and confidence in men have borne fruit.

It is precisely this sense of right that will take generations of actual living to achieve in most women. It is the cry of the age that women have *not* walked the earth as though they owned it, have *not* expected they would find and take into themselves the goods of life. Therefore, they have not assimilated their own experience; therefore, whatever might be the characteristic "femaleness" of their working selves remains at this moment unexplored and unarticulated.

One day there may develop a practice of law, medicine, economics, or science some of whose traits or values may be traced to the influence of vast numbers of women having entered the discipline, but today is not the day. Right now, the women who rise are those who have identified with the aggressor, so to speak; those who have learned how to be, not from consultation with the innermost self but from mimicry of how it was done by the only ones doing it: the men who alone possessed the sole visible means for becoming a thinking, acting human being.

My answer to the original question then—do women do science differently—is no. I asked many scientists (men and women) if they saw a difference in the practice of science between the sexes. All replied: "No. Once they get there women work exactly like men." I myself was unable to observe women organizing their thoughts differently, or asking different kinds of scientific questions, or applying different methods of investigation.

But feminism itself—as a movement, an idea, a piece of social thought—constitutes an intrusive influence in science today. Something new is happening in the profession because of it. All these women coming into science in ever-growing numbers, and bringing their "live issues" with them for the first time in history, have forced on the profession a self-consciousness regarding its own power politics. This consciousness is slowly bringing science into greater consonance with the social ideas that are changing the internal self-description of women, and of men, everywhere; ideas whose final reverberations are yet to be felt but whose strength can easily be observed altering behavior both public and private, values both personal and avowed, old definitions of what enriches and what atrophies a life as well as those of what is to be admired and respected, adored or worshipped. These ideas have raised anew the question of the century: In the name of what, and for whose benefit, is *this* definition of a participant in the enterprise upheld? Are *these* particular practices condoned or insisted upon? Is *this* rigidity of allegiances enforced?

Because of feminism, a slow but visible change is taking place in the shared conviction among scientists of how a scientist works, and therefore who a scientist *is*. Inflexibly held notions about the relation between traditional practices and the quality of the work are beginning to give way beneath the mounting pressure of scientists who are not doing science "the way it has always been done," but who are obviously doing it nonetheless.

There is in science today a complete microcosm of the sociology of feminism that has grown up in American life over the past fifteen years. Among women scientists there are radical, liberal, and conservative feminists, as well as open fellow travelers and secret sympathizers. An atmosphere of receptivity has evolved so that the questions feminism raises are met if not with eager acceptance at least with grudging consideration, if not stimulated response certainly not blind rejection. It is the rare woman scientist who feels she can simply ignore or deny the question of women in science, no matter how intellectually or psychologically distant from it she may feel; there is embarrassment rather than self-assurance if one is not a partisan. The issue of women in science is alive in the profession. Those who address the issue directly are numerous, and their positions are endless.

A number of women scientists have grown disaffected and have become radical feminists, but these women have not left the profession. They remain self-described scientists whose passion is now political rather than scientific. To many of their colleagues their presence in science is a source of scorn and chagrin, to others their presence is a harbinger. To themselves, they are gadflies, dissidents, catalysts. They would no more dream of leaving science because they are disaffected from research itself than would a true religious who longs to see a corrupt church returned to its original state of grace and promise think of leaving the church.

A former research associate in biology says: "When I became a feminist the scientists acted as though I had betrayed them. But feminism politicized me. Every professor in my department was a white male. Every secretary, technician, and research associate was female or black. They prepared the young men to go on, but me never. Do you know how many I groomed for a career in science? But they expected me to stay there forever, just as I was. When I realized this I couldn't go on. . . . But I have loved science. I love it still. I couldn't just leave it. Now I teach science to women four nights a week at a local women's center. I participate as a scientist in women's studies programs all over the state, I lecture on the political nature of scientific investigation in this country. My life feels integrated for the first time in years."

Another scientist, a forty-two-year-old tenured physiologist at an Eastern state university, also disaffected from the work itself, describes her past life in science thus: "When two men meet at a scientific conference they exchange credentials in a subtle but well understood manner, and proceed to speak together as though competence is assumed. I always felt I was *approached* as though I were not legitimate, as though it was assumed I was an *in*competent until I proved otherwise. Walking into a conference, speaking at a meeting, attending a seminar, it was always the same. As the years passed the strain mounted, and in time I felt it was suffocating me. Then I began to think: I wanted to do science so I'd gain pleasure from my work and respect from my contemporaries. I saw I was never going to gain the latter, and then I began to feel it would be the same with the former. Working for the sake of work alone, I could never see that. I wanted a whole life."

By the time she was granted tenure the physiologist had in effect stopped doing science, but she retained her professorship, and she goes through the motions of being a scientist: She teaches, she runs a lab, she applies for and receives grants. Her real life, though, is the women's movement, women's studies programs the ever-present dilemma of how to bring women scientists into a professional life equal to that of men.

Sarah Griswold, the fifty-six-year-old Ivy League chemist, is also a scientist turned feminist. She has not been absorbed by scientific questions for a good six or seven years now. A convert of the first order to the primacy of the women's movement, Sarah attends every feminist conference and meeting in the country, teaches science-and-women's-issues, is part of a feminist publishing collective, lectures wherever and whenever she can as an antagonist of current scientific practices, and speaks openly of the discriminatory nature of the profession.

Many women in science resent Sarah bitterly. The struggle for her tenure was a significant one, and her desertion from research is felt to be a betrayal. But Sarah refuses to shoulder the burden of guilt being laid on her. "Look how many men are bored to death with science after twenty or thirty years in it, but they keep on plodding along at it, wishing, just wishing they could find something new in life to do. Well, I've found it! Science is not more important than equality for women. In fact, if there is no equality for women, pretty soon there will be no science. The profession *must* change. To this I am as committed as I once was to asking scientific questions."

Women like Sarah Griswold and the physiologist represent a curious extremity of a general condition: the real weariness many academics feel by the time they are granted tenure. They demonstrate the common truth that tenure is not a stimulation to do new and good work, but a relaxation of the guard against an exhaustion that has unconsciously already set in for most academics. The women incorporate an open anger into their weariness, and their feminist politics has given them a context within which disappointment and belligerence become tools of useful obsession.

It is important that these women have not simply walked away from science, that they have stayed to become the goading, prodding, political crazies of the profession. They don't *do* science, but they are in a position to act as catalysts for angry discussion. They call knowledgeable attention to the position of women in science; they keep the issue alive, force the question on everyone, cause discomfort, defensiveness, denunciation, inquiry. They add osmotically to an atmosphere that pulls together feminism, science, and social ideas, to an insistence that all are related. These people do not have direct influence today but they are being heard by those who will have power tomorrow.

More to the point right now is a significant *other* minority in science: the women who are dedicated scientists and who do not necessarily call themselves feminists but who, in ever-growing self-consciousness, bear less and less resemblance to the silent, anonymous, unintrusive lady scientist of yesterday, the scientists Vivian Davidson was referring to when she said, "They're so glad to be allowed into the club they don't want to make waves." These are women who refuse in the name of love *or* work to push themselves out of shape, to cut off some parts, atrophy others, pinch and silence and muffle; the women for whom doing what Annie Morris did (wearing a lab coat two sizes larger so that no one would know she was pregnant) is now unthinkable. These women embody the mainstream effect of feminism on science.

Among these women the question of having families and still being a serious full-time scientist constitutes a major dilemma that has resulted in an open debate. It is a question central to feminist concerns, one that will be grappled with for generations by those who know that ultimately all people must share in the world enterprise, and all people must parent the children. The scientists of whom I now speak have brought this problem—alive in every sphere of working life in America today—into science, and they are forcing on their profession the continuous reminder that attention must be paid now to the meaning of intimate relations in a working person's life; something no scientist has ever had to attend to before.

The debate itself reflects the heterogeneous composition of women scientists. It is not at all that there is a single monolithic view to which "women in science" subscribe. Far from it. There are as many views as there are women to hold them. This multiplicity is evidence of the vigor of the argument and the depth of its possible consequence. Again, because the case is being debated so vociferously, the question is nourished, made to grow, allowed to worm its way slowly into the social reality of science and scientists. One day all scientists will think very differently than they do now about the relation between family life and working life. That change in thought will have been arrived at because these women are arguing "among themselves" today.

Alice Hawthorne assumes a position in that argument that is as inflammatory as it is unyielding. She is a thirty-seven-year-old tenured physicist at a university famous for its scientific research. Tall, rangy, upper class, an intellectual Katharine Hepburn, Hawthorne's characteristic pose is held while sitting behind her desk, one trousered leg raised up onto the seat of her chair, an elbow propped on the knee of the raised leg, a cigarette in the raised hand, the free hand pushing her glasses up onto the bridge of her fine nose or running roughly through short, thick, springy hair. The face is haggard, the voice throaty, tired, self-assured.

She was the student of a Nobel laureate. From the beginning physics was a drug, a dream, an entirety of life to her: She was in the lab till three in the morning four nights out of seven. She still believes that is how it must be. She describes a graduate student of hers, a young woman whom she says is an excellent physicist, but for whom she does not predict a life in science. The student is going to be married soon. Alice says with awe in her voice: "She's as interested in her upcoming wedding as she is in the experiments she's doing. I can't believe it." Alice shakes her head no. "She'll never make it. That's not what it's all about. At this point in her life she should have nothing—nothing—on her mind but the lab. She should be *killing* herself with work. There should be absolutely nothing else in her head."

Alice herself cannot put in the same hours in the lab just now that she has put in for years. Her struggle to gain tenure at this university was monumental, and it has tired her tremendously. She explains that her department has a Nobel laureate who disliked and set himself against her. According to Alice, this laureate is "the most loathsome human being I've ever known. He steals from everybody and he doesn't even know he's doing it. He's the kind of man whose mind is a rapid synthesizer of other people's ideas. He listens to something you're thinking about, almost musing about, an idea only half thought out, and he immediately sees its implications, sees where it fits into something he's been working on, and he snatches it, and the next thing you know, with absolutely no mention given to *you,* he's presenting your ideas in a paper as though they're part of his own work, and always have been.

"This practice became intolerable to me. I became so nervous and paranoid I didn't want to speak to anyone about my work. And it's that way with everyone else here. The great intellectual atmosphere of the great research university! What a bad joke that is. The atmosphere here is terrible. Silent, isolated, cutthroat. There is no intellectual exchange. Everyone distrusts everyone else, no one will support anyone. It's dreadful. And *he's* the worst of the lot. I fought him every inch of the way.

"When it came time for tenure—and by this time I'd done work of an international nature—he simply said, 'I don't want her here.' I give him credit. He didn't say, 'She's a fool, and her work is no good.' He said, 'She's very good, and her work is very good, but I don't like her, I don't want her in the department, and if you give her tenure I'll leave.'

"I couldn't believe this was happening to me. I just couldn't believe it. I walked around in a daze. And then I called *my* laureate. I had called him a number of times before when I was miserable and had said I was leaving. Each time he had said, 'Stay where you are. That's an order.' Now I called him and said, 'It's all over. I can't fight anymore.' He said, 'You'll stay there and we'll fight. If they don't give you tenure we'll sue.' 'On what grounds?' I asked. 'I'll sue him for having stolen some of my ideas. It's all right. Half the people in physics feel he's stolen something from them. But don't worry, it won't come to that.' And it didn't. What my laureate did was plant the rumor in a few well-placed ears that if I didn't get tenure he was going to sue the university. And that did it. I got tenure. And the bastard didn't leave, unfortunately."

Alice lights a cigarette, pushes her glasses up onto the bridge of her nose, runs her hand tiredly through her hair. "Imagine what it means if you're a woman with no connections? Here I am, with one of the most influential men in science today fighting for me, and look what *I* had to go through. Imagine if I was just an ordinary woman with no one behind her? How much *more* one must have the energy and freedom to fight? Imagine if I had had a husband and family to take care of during this time? Forget it. I could never have done it."

Alice Hawthorne has very definite ideas about being a woman in science, ideas that grow out of experience, conviction, and cast of mind. She says, in essence, the only way to be a woman in science is to forget about being a woman. It is impossible to live in the world of contemporary professional science, and rise to the top of the profession, and still be a woman in old-fashioned terms (that is, have a family). She says it can't be done, and points out that the majority of women in science are unmarried, or married with no children, or divorced with no intention of remarrying.

In 1976 Alice wrote a now-infamous article in her alumni journal in which she expressed these views openly and strongly, and added that the best thing for women in science was to face this truth squarely, and then make whatever decision they had to make.

Alice Hawthorne's views (those of a nineteenth-century feminist) are shared by many women, and welcomed by even more men ("See? We told you there was good reason why things have always been this way. Here is proof that the terms are immutable"), but her article raised a storm among many other scientists who said "Nonsense. Not only nonsense, this kind of thinking is retrograde and dangerous to us all." Among those most vocal on the matter was Andrea Livewright.

Andrea wrote an article in *her* alumni journal in which she declared Alice Hawthorne's views unacceptable. She said the points Alice was making supported a view and a philosophy of life that was now intolerable, that the partial and stunted lives which resulted from such a myopic sense of what was required to be a scientist were to be avoided not applauded, that anyone who thought a life in the lab without the humanizing effects of a family was worthwhile was wrong-headed, and that what Alice was really talking about was participating in, rather than challenging, the cruel and crippling effects of Ivy League competitiveness; that it was not a matter of doing great science or not doing great science, it was more a matter of the ongoingness of a self-appointed, self-sustaining elitism that often did *not* earn itself out intellectually. Yes, it was true that great scientists emerged from the Ivy League, but it was also true that fine and often great science was being done by people working in other places, under conditions they now prized as much as they had once prized the elite connection. Again, Andrea insisted, it was not really the work in the lab Alice Hawthorne's views addressed, it was a set of prejudices, arrogant and self-serving, that had not been reviewed in a hundred years; working in the lab ninety hours a week often had more to do with satisfying the nasty requirements of a careerism modeled on and shaped by that very male competitiveness that Merton had described so well; a competitiveness designed to eliminate many kinds of men, and certainly designed to eliminate all women. All this Andrea Livewright said in *her* rebuttal. To which Sharlene George said *amen*.

Sharlene George has views as strong as Alice Hawthorne's on the matter of its taking ninety hours a week in the lab to be a first-rate scientist. "That is really nonsense," she says curtly. "What it takes is being very smart, and very well organized, and if you're *that*, you can do what you have to do between nine in the morning and six in the evening, and still go home and have a family life. The men who have turned science into an eighteen-hour-a day macho life have done so because they weren't smart enough to do it otherwise, and because it serves their real values which don't include relationships with their wives and children. Any man who's got a wife at home whose life is like that of a servant to the great man, I *despise*. I can hardly talk to those people.

"And I can't help it, I don't think it's my prejudice working, but when I look around it seems to me that the worst ones— the ones who are making an identity out of always being in the lab, never being home with their families—are absolutely not the smartest scientists at all.

"Look at it this way. My chairman is a brilliant fellow, but he's not really interested in science anymore. He's interested in travel, theater, I don't know *what* the hell he's interested in, half the time he's not here at all. But when he *is* here, he's invariably doing interesting and potentially important work. That man operates at ten percent of his capacity. He's working on a ninety-percent margin. Now the guy down the hall, he's a competent scientist. Not brilliant at all. Just hardworking and industrious. He's in the lab ninety hours a week and, believe me, he needs every one of those ninety hours to accomplish the little that he does accomplish. He's working on a ten-percent margin. Me, I'm somewhere between my chairman and the guy down the hall. I have to be here every day, and put in a good eight hours in the lab, but I don't have to be here ninety hours a week to produce good work.

"Max Perutz once told Horace Judson that other scientists sneered at Jim Watson for playing tennis and chasing girls—until Watson solved the problem of the double helix. Perutz said Watson always knew it wasn't the amount of work you did, it was the quality of the work that counted. That story is told to demonstrate genius at work, but it could have been, and should have been, told of all scientists. Every scientist works differently and that difference has *got* to be acknowledged now. It works against women not to have it acknowledged.

"I always knew I'd have it all. Science, family, the works. I *wanted* it. I was willing to work hard for it. I knew I could do it. And many women can do it. And will do it. Because more and more, *they* want it, too. And I want to see it happen not just for women, but for men also, for everyone. *Everyone* should be a parent to his or her children. *Everyone* should have a family life, an intimate marriage. My god, without that you're half a person. Why should anyone think that you have to be half a person in order to do science?"

*   *   *

Jacob Bronowski—the Polish-English mathematician, historian, philosopher—loved the idea of science with a rare expansiveness and generosity. He held his view of the primacy of scientific thought in an easy embrace that included respect and admiration for the greatness of literature, philosophy, invention, and politics. He was devoted to the intimate relation between civilization and science because it gave him the happy reassurance of historic understanding. Bronowski never lost sight of the large idea of society, and he never forgot that science and society were inextricably related. He also knew how that relationship worked.

In *The Common Sense of Science*—one of the many small books Bronowski left behind when he died in 1974—he said: "I have looked at the ideas of science always in the setting of their times. From year to year they grow larger until at last the outline is quite changed. And the growth does not go on in empty space, it does not even go on in an abstract space where there is nothing but ideas. It goes on in the world, the rational and empirical world." Later on, in this same book, in an astonishing throwaway line, Bronowski remarked casually: "The trend of science is made by the needs of society: navigation before the 18th century, manufacture thereafter; and in our age I believe the liberation of personality."

In the last few hundred years we have all loved art with a capital A, science with a capital S, revolution with a capital R. This love has been part of an organic view of life, homogeneous and hierarchic, which holds that work of the mind or the spirit is to be worshipped as one worships at the shrine of a Holy Being because one believes that holiness (that is, the state of grace) is without, and one hopes that if one is obedient, and serves the Being properly, one will be granted salvation. We have worshipped at the shrine of the Muse, the Discovery, the Analysis in much the same way, given ourselves with passion to the thing that is bigger than ourselves, if not to insure salvation, certainly to save ourselves from the void.

In this world of reverence for that which is bigger than ourselves, all else being equal men have ritually been the primary worshippers at the shrine of Art or Intellect while women have, just as ritually, been servants to the worshippers of Art or Intellect. All have participated willingly in this scheme; no one has had to be coerced, neither men nor women. All have accepted this division as immutable because all have believed that if the prescription were changed, the ritual altered, the ceremony challenged, The Great Enterprise would be endangered; that the kingdom of spirit and intellect, art and revolution, creativity and transformation would be lost to us if The Great Work were not performed in precisely the way we had come to believe it must be performed, and by precisely those we had come to believe could alone do it well. We would have failed to serve properly, and that failure would have sent us spinning into the void. (It is precisely this anxiety that Dorothy Dinnerstein traces in *The Mermaid and the Minotaur,* her great work on the meaning of the sexual arrangement—the agreement between men and women that men will be whole persons, and women half-persons, out of the common fear that without the arrangement the anchors will come loose, and all of us will fall in meaningless space.)

But something new is happening in our time, and especially in our place. We are living through a moment when the idea of self-possession is replacing the idea of The Great Work. This new idea has taken strong hold in thousands of people struggling to lead serious lives. It is an idea diametrically opposed to ritual acceptance of The Enterprise as holy, and the notion that people must arrange themselves in hierarchic relation to it; an idea that posits: "The enterprise is not greater than we are, and none of us should be sacrificed to it. It is, after all, our creation. It is there to entertain and delight, instruct and nourish *all* of us. We must come into a more equitable relation, one to the other"; an idea that has, of course, been growing itself—alone and in the dark—for a long time now.

I. I. Rabi said mockingly to me, "Well? The doors are open now to women, and where are the great scientists?" Not only was the question mean-spirited and arrogant—the men who spoke openly of touching God often secretly believed they were God—it was the wrong question. I don't think Bronowski would have asked that question. I think Bronowski would have said: "The point is not where are the great women scientists. The point is now that the doors are open let us see where they have *been,* and what we can learn from it." Then, I think, with the light beaming from his glasses and with that rich, perfected sense of wonder in his voice, Bronowski would have said: "Imagine! All those women working for a hundred years in obscurity and isolation, without reward or recognition, hanging on by their fingernails, sustaining daily humiliation, just to do science! Ah, I was right! The greatest discovery of scientists is science itself. How expressive it is in its nature, and what a fundamental human activity it *is!* These women have reminded me."

Indeed. The history of women in science speaks brilliantly to the love of doing science that lay behind the worship of Science. This history "reminds" us of that which is repeatedly lost and forgotten: that there is a special relation between the gathering of knowledge and the need to feel the life within ourselves; and that, concomitantly, there is a live quality present in the enterprise when the gathering of knowledge and the sense of self are held in balance, and absent when the balance is lost.

Now that we are moving into a time when the idea of the expressive self (or as Bronowski put it "the liberation of per-

sonality") is gaining dominion, women scientists—by virtue
of their cumulative history and ever-growing numbers—are
strongly associated with the recovery of this simple, profound
truth. As thousands of women go steadily about their business, being themselves and doing science, they are in effect
saying, "Science must come down off that pedestal we could
never have climbed. The love of science is immutable, the
shrine to Science is not. If we are not sacrificed on an un-
worthy altar today we will perhaps lead science back to being a source of inner renewal tomorrow."

These scientists are able to speak so because history is with
them, and because science needs them to say it. This insistence
of the women might very well return "wholeness" to science.
The fragmented sense of the profession that older scientists at-
test to will probably disappear as social change is absorbed,
and out of the absorption there emerges a new integration and
a new intellectual energy.

The fear of men like Rabi that the new social ideas will
cause "great" science to disintegrate is a piece of dogma,
groundless and anxiety-ridden; where there is dogma there is
the secret conviction that if one relaxes one's hold on the pre-
scriptive way of doing things, one may find oneself holding
nothing: a wisp of parchment, feathers, dust. More than most
responses to organized experience, dogma indicates that one
no longer trusts that there is live truth in the experience itself.

But science, as Bronowski knew, grows out of a compulsion
in the human spirit to understand, to make sense of the world
around us. Such a compulsion is stronger than intellectual or
social doctrine, stronger than the institutions that come to
house it, stronger even than "insufficient" practitioners of the
disciplines it gives rise to. If the compulsion is stifled it fights
for air, if it is perverted it struggles to right itself, if it is killed
it is—in time—reborn. It is a force that must be recognized
and honored. There is no need to build shrines to it, or to sac-

rifice lives to it. It is not something holy, a gift of grace bestowed from without. It is a human characteristic, inborn, always there, always ready to reassert itself.

The idea that the expressive self is defined through engagement, that engagement is an act of self-creation, that self-creation is an instrument of discovery—this idea should be greeted with cheers and enthusiasm. It is an idea that reminds and revitalizes, shakes thought and behavior out of settled patterns, startles us into asking once more: "Who *are* we? And what are we doing here?"

Feminism is a vigorous and potent contributor to this atmosphere of animation and renewal. Neither manifesto, doctrine, or program, feminism is a way of seeing things, an instrument of analysis that brings into disturbing question what we thought we had settled long ago. In the simple act of announcing: "We are not as we have been described," thousands of women have forced us to look with new eyes on a piece of experience we assumed was thoroughly understood. We have now had to see that we haven't understood it at all, we have mistaken its meaning entirely, and we have had to rethink a whole set of fundamental relationships. Rethinking, we have discovered that a great deal of "data" we had not been able to account for properly in the past suddenly made new sense. The new sense had consequences.

Looking at old behaviors under the strong light of a different analytic lens has changed more than the interpretations of the behaviors themselves. As women have described themselves anew, the environment in which they are describing has become new as well. In seeing what has always been there to be seen, but which we have not been able or ready to see until now, feminism mimics the analytic process that is the spirit of the age. Inevitably, to describe anew is to transform.

Science—which also, ultimately, asks: "Who are we, and

what are we doing here?"—is the original model for all such activity. There is a poster to be found on laboratory walls all over the country that depicts a huge eye surrounded by darkness, and below the eye the words: "To see what everybody else has seen, and think what nobody else has thought." The quote is from Albert Szent-Gyorgyi, but it might have come from Newton. Science, like feminism, looks at that which has always been there to be seen, and as it "sees" for the first time it describes a new world.

Feminism and science share vital characteristics today. Both are filled with urgency and conviction, both are observing intently, both are concentrated on demystifying the self and the environment, recovering the truths of the life within. Women in science—both separately and collectively—stir the contemporary imagination. In their hyphenated identity is captured the pain and excitement of a culture struggling to mature.

A SELECTED BIBLIOGRAPHY

1. *The Eighth Day of Creation,* Horace Freeland Judson (New York: Simon & Schuster, 1979).
   This book remains, for me, the most comprehensive piece of scientific writing. It captures brilliantly the feel of doing science while leading the nonscientific reader through the intricate maze of a great scientific discovery.
2. *Experiencing Science,* Jeremy Bernstein (New York: Basic Books, 1978).
   A series of wonderfully written profiles of scientists (among them I. I. Rabi, Johannes Kepler, and Lewis Thomas) and of scientific discoveries and dilemmas (among *them* a problematic review of Anne Sayre's book on Rosalind Franklin.
3. *Rosalind Franklin and DNA,* Anne Sayre (New York: W. W. Norton & Co., 1975).
   Written as a corrective to Watson's portrait of Rosalind Franklin in *The Double Helix,* this book is unsatisfying in that its tone is so defensive the reader comes to distrust its account and interpretation of the crucial events it is describing. Nevertheless, it is a necessary document in the unhappy and disturbing affair of Rosalind Franklin's contribution to the discovery of the structure of DNA.
4. *The Sociology of Science,* Robert K. Merton (Chicago: University of Chicago Press, 1973).
   A collection of papers, written over many years, that deal with the idea of knowledge in general and of scientific knowledge in particular, the normative structure of the profession of science, the rewards system and the method of evaluation in

science. If the subject of professional science is of interest to a reader, these papers are stimulating and pleasurable to read.

5. *Life: The Unfinished Experiment,* S. E. Luria (New York: Scribners, 1973).

A long essay, by one of the great biologists of our time, that explains the evolution of modern genetics in clear, always interesting language. Luria very quietly brings the untrained reader along with him into the meaning and excitement of molecular biology, an achievement of no small matter.

6. *Advice to a Young Scientist,* Peter Medawar (New York: Harper & Row, 1979).

Medawar writes as though he imagines himself a scientific Lord Chesterfield instructing his intellectual sons and daughters in the art of becoming a civilized scientist.

7. *Genes and Gender II* (Staten Island, New York: The Gordian Press, 1979).

The second in a series of papers on sociological notions of gender differences. Written and collected by a group of feminist scientists, these papers are all intelligent and stimulating.

8. *An Imagined World,* June Goodfield (New York: Harper & Row, 1981).

Through an interweaving of letters, tape-recorded conversations, and narrative explanation, we follow a forty-year-old cell biologist through five years of her scientific life. We learn what sort of a human being the scientist is, what science means to her, how she works inside that meaning. Written by a skilled science writer, this is the kind of book future scientists will recall as having been influential in their decision to do science.

9. *The Lives of a Cell,* Lewis Thomas (New York: Viking Press, 1974).

These now famous essays, built around the conceit that the earth is like a single cell, are the work of a poetic scientist whose sense of wonder has never deserted him. Invaluable reading for anyone writing about science or scientists.

10. *Women Look at Biology Looking at Women,* Hubbard, Heni-

fin, Fried, eds. (Cambridge, Massachusetts: Schenkman Publishing Co., 1979).
A collection of feminist critiques that attempts to show that much more social bias has influenced scientific theory and practice than is commonly understood.

11. *Fair Science, Jonathan* R. Cole (New York: The Free Press, 1979).
A statistical analysis by a sociologist of science that seeks to "measure" the position of women scientists in the American scientific community. Cole's findings led him to at least two conclusions that aroused the angry protest of many women scientists—that women select themselves out of science, but if they stick with it the meritocracy works for them.

12. *The Coming of the Golden Age and the End of Progress,* Gunther Stent (New York: Doubleday, 1969).
A bilious little book by a disappointed and conservative man whose thesis is that the counterculture movement in America ushered in the end of "progress" as we have always known it, and that contemporary science reflects this intellectual demise: All the great questions in science have now been asked and answered, there is nothing more to learn, scientists are now doing busy work, filling in the spaces inside an outline that has long ago been drawn and now stands fully revealed.

13. *Science and Human Values,* J. Bronowski (New York: Harper & Row, 1972); *The Common Sense of Science,* J. Bronowski (Cambridge, Massachusetts: Harvard University Press, 1978); *Magic, Science and Civilization,* J. Bronowski (New York: Columbia University Press, 1978). Nothing could be further from Stent's books than these little books of Bronowski's: essays suffused with love of science as a spirit of inquiry that continues, throughout the centuries, to influence and extend our idea of who we are, and what we are doing here.

14. *Uneasy Careers and Intimate Lives: Women in Science 1789– 1979,* Pnina G. Abir-am and Dorinda Outram (New Brunswick, New Jersey: Rutgers University Press, 1987). This collection of pioneering studies of women in science pays spe-

cial attention to the mutual impact of family life and scientific careers. The contributors address historical changes, gender image, national differences, opening opportunities, and women's levels of awareness about the role of gender in science.

INDEX